Dependent Origination

The 12 Links

Dukkha (Suffering)

By Delson Armstrong

Editing and layout: David Johnson

Imprint: Independently published

Other Books by Delson Armstrong

"A Mind Without Craving", Netherlands, 2021

"Dependent Origination-12 book Series", USA, 2022

"Bhikkhus, there are these Four Noble Truths. What four? The noble truth of suffering, the noble truth of the origin of suffering, the noble truth of the cessation of suffering, the noble truth of the way leading to the cessation of suffering.

Saccasamyutta Sn 56.13(3) Aggregates

Contents

Introduction

The purpose of this booklet is to help the truth seeker to understand the concept of ***Dependent Origination***. This is the most essential idea to be understood on your journey to Nibbāna. The Buddha used the term *paṭicca samuppāda,* which is Pāli for dependent origination. When one understands Dependent Origination one understands himself/herself and the world. It is truly the answer to the question of "Who am I?"

This is a 12-part series of small books - one for each of the 12 links. This is the first book on the 12th link of Dukkha. Later all these booklets will be combined into a larger book or books.

But first, the definition of Dependent Origination from the Buddha.

Dependent Origination

Saṃyutta Nikaya 12.1.1

"Monks, I will teach you dependent origination. Listen to that and attend closely, I will speak."–"Yes, venerable sir," those monks replied.

The Blessed One said this:

"And what, students, is dependent origination? With ignorance as condition, volitional formations come to be; with volitional formations as condition, consciousness; with consciousness as condition, name-and-form; with name-and-form as condition, the six sense bases; with the six sense bases as condition, contact; with contact as condition, feeling; with feeling as condition, craving; with craving as condition, clinging; with clinging as condition, existence; with existence as condition, birth; with birth as condition, aging-and-death, sorrow, lamentation, pain, displeasure, and despair come to be. Such is the origin of this whole mass of suffering. This, students, is called dependent origination.

"But with the remainderless fading away and cessation of ignorance comes cessation of volitional formations; with the cessation of volitional formations, cessation of consciousness; with the cessation of consciousness, cessation of name-and-form; with the cessation of name-and-form, cessation of the six sense bases; with the cessation of the six sense bases, cessation of contact; with the cessation of contact, cessation of feeling; with the cessation of feeling, cessation of craving; with the cessation of craving, cessation of clinging; with the cessation of clinging, cessation of existence; with the cessation of existence, cessation of birth; with the cessation of birth, aging-and-death, sorrow, lamentation, pain, displeasure, and despair cease. Such is the cessation of this whole mass of suffering."

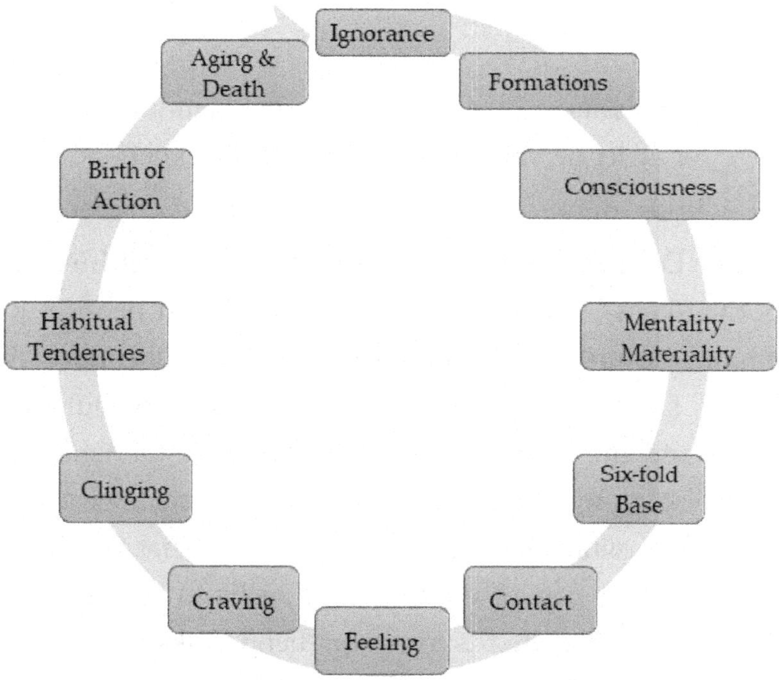

Dukkha

I. Dukkha

Idaṁ kho pana, bhikkhave, dukkhaṁ ariyasaccaṁ—

Now this, bhikkhus, is the noble truth of suffering

- SN 56.11, Dhammacakkappavattana Sutta

Dukkha is the First Noble Truth. It must be understood and in order for it to be understood, it must be experienced. All beings whose minds are bound and tainted by Saṃsāra experience Dukkha, whether or not they want to, and whether or not they know it. Dukkha is often glossed over because it is something the untrained and restless mind is uncomfortable with when faced with this concrete reality. To know Dukkha is to understand the First Noble Truth. To see it for what it is proves to be more valuable than trying to push it away and suppressing it, which causes further Dukkha. That is why the Buddha says that part of the task that needs to be done for a mind to be fully liberated is to comprehend Dukkha. With this task laid before one by the Buddha, one then trains to comprehend it and in the process of reviewing the mind that had laid down the burden, one assesses that indeed the mind has fully comprehended Dukkha.

Having seen this as one of the tasks to be completed, let us begin from the end of one cycle of Dependent Origination. Now although Dukkha is a broad overarching container of the component of Jarāmaraṇa, which is in fact the twelfth and final link in Dependent Origination, let us consider for the moment that to understand Dukkha and it various composites is as important if not more important than understanding Jarāmaraṇa alone, for the simple facts laid out above – that to liberate the mind, the first step is to know Dukkha in a structured and complete manner born from a methodical and systematic review of its factors.

Meaning of Dukkha

Dukkha has numerous meanings depending on the context. Within the Nikāyas themselves, Dukkha is equated with Identity (Sakkāya), with Rebirth (Jāti), and with the other components, which we will explore in this chapter. Dukkha is a compound word arising first from the prefix Du, which means bad or difficult. Kkha in Pali arises from the Sanskrit Stha, which means that which is stable, that which is steady and dependable and will provide comfort and ease.

Another way to see Dukkha is to understand its diametrical opposite from a linguistic perspective and that word would be

Sukha. Interestingly, here the suffix, Kha, means an opening or a hole, and Su means good or easy. This is in reference to the ancient Indian understanding of an effective chariot with wheels that ran smoothly and swiftly, because of a good axle hole through which the axle could function in an easy manner, providing a comfortable ride for the passengers. From that context, one can see that Dukkha is this fundamental imperfection of the chariot due to an ineffective axle hole. Extending this understanding to the wheel of Saṃsāra, we see that it is imperfect because of its fundamental quality of possessing Dukkha.

Of course, in conversational Sanskrit or Pali, Sukha means happiness or comfort, a sense of well-being. Therefore, Dukkha is that sense of dread or unease, a certain unsatisfying quality to something and in the dispensation of the Buddha, Dukkha here specifically would refer to the intrinsic quality of existence for a number of reasons, the primary of which include its impermanent and conditioned nature. Because it implies so many meanings that one's mind may incline towards a particular dimension of this word, which could include "suffering," "pain," "dissatisfaction," "instability" "prone to change," "unhappiness" "grief," "unease," "imperfection," and so much more, it would be apt to consolidate all of them under this one word "Dukkha" in Pali.

Dukkha-Dukkha

Dukkha-Dukkha here refers to the Dukkha of the First Noble Truth. That is as the Buddha explains in DN 22, Mahāsatipaṭṭhāna Sutta -

Jātipi dukkhā, jarāpi dukkhā, maraṇampi dukkhaṁ, sokaparidevadukkhadomanassupāyāsāpi dukkhā, appiyehi sampayogopi dukkho, piyehi vippayogopi dukkho, yampicchaṁ na labhati tampi dukkhaṁ, saṅkhittena pañcupādānakkhandhāpi dukkhā

Birth is suffering, aging is suffering, death is suffering, sorrow, lamentation, pain, sadness, and distress are suffering. Union with what is displeasing is suffering; separation from what is pleasing is suffering; not to get what one wants is suffering; in brief, the five aggregates subject to clinging are suffering.

Dukkha-Dukkha is most apparent in Saṃsāra. Even animals have the capacity to comprehend Dukkha-Dukkha through fear, hunger, violence, oppression, disease, famine, death, and even grief. If you've ever seen or known the pet of someone who had passed away, you may have noticed that the animal was grief-stricken at the absence of their loved one, aware enough to know of their demise. This Dukkha-Dukkha begins from childbirth and is experienced through growing pains, sickness, anxieties and worry, restlessness and lust, hatred and shame, and other unwholesome reactions when one reaches adolescence and adulthood. Finally old age and the remorse of or an attachment to things, memories, situations, and relationships long gone as one reflects on the deathbed may become the last thoughts infused by Dukkha until one succumbs to the inevitability of death and the end of that particular lifetime.

Vipariṇāma Dukkha

This Dukkha is related to the temporary nature of all conditioned things, which are subject to change. It includes union with what is displeasing, separation from what is pleasing and not getting what one wants. Vipariṇāma, in fact, means change or transformation. It's the Dukkha one experiences having taken the first bite of one's favorite meal and when the tastebuds are saturated with flavors, they are unable to replicate that same feeling of deliciousness with the second bite. It's when you go into the hot shower on a cold day and feel the initial warmth of the water, which gradually the body gets used to and you no longer feel the initial moment of comfort and relief when the water first touched your skin.

When you know that you have to go back to work after the weekend and that feeling of dread arises, this is Vipariṇāma Dukkha. Or when you expect your vacation to begin but your flight is delayed and ultimately canceled. In short, any time one expects something to happen a certain way and it doesn't, when one experiences pleasure and it fades away, or when one tries to hold onto something that is bound to pass away, like holding onto the memory or trying to replicate the feeling of one's first kiss but it never really feels the same way again, or when one's relationship is unexpectedly broken and one tries to fix it but to no avail, one experiences Vipariṇāma Dukkha. A more supramundane example would be when one experiences a certain jhāna and its factors but then they fade away due to lack of collectedness or hindrances arising. This Dukkha is the result of not realizing the impermanent nature of all conditioned experiences that arose from prior causes and circumstances.

Saṅkhāra Dukkha

This Dukkha is the most subtle and yet the most pervasive. Saṅkhāra Dukkha is the Dukkha of all things that are conditioned. Saṅkhāra refers to formations, which in of themselves are conditioned by prior experiences and choices. Therefore, such Dukkha can be the effect of negative choices one made in the past which is now experienced as a result of not understanding and of taking things personal. This Dukkha arises from Avijjā or Ignorance, from which one identifies with experiences without mindfulness and thus creates the potential for further conditioned experiences.

Such Dukkha is experienced through the five aggregates of vedanā (feeling), saññā (perception), saṅkhāra (formations), and vijñāna (consciousness), and therefore it is certainly more psychological than physical. It's the dread of existence that is unavoidable when one starts to reflect on one's choices and life. It can manifest into nihilism where one becomes depressed and anxious, considering life to be meaningless and can devolve into philosophical pessimism, creating dullness and apathy in the mind and even an existential crisis. It includes the feeling that nothing can truly satisfy the mind or body according to one's expectations. One's very thoughts are Dukkha.

The Insight into Dukkha

Dukkha is best understood as a characteristic of existence. Once this is accepted, meaning it has been reviewed through one's own experience with complete nibbidā, or disenchantment, and virāga, or dispassion, then one no longer has any fear or aversion towards Dukkha, nor any other reaction that can cause the mind to create further Dukkha for itself. The mind becomes tranquil and light, filled with wisdom through the process of seeing. This process is attenuated by the tool of Yoniso Manasikāra or Attention Rooted in Reality. With such a mind inclined to the reality of the situation as it is, one applies the natural process born from collectedness, which is samādhi, and this brings about yathā-bhūta-ñāna-dassana, which is seeing Reality as it is without filters, projections, craving, personalizing or ignorance. Having seen this, nibbidā and virāga naturally arise. From this comes the seeing of the tilakkhaṇa, the three characteristics, which are Anicca, Dukkha, and Anatta.

The seeing of Dukkha therefore is dependent on understanding Anicca, the impermanent nature of all things that are bound by Saṃsāra. Anicca comes from the prefix A, which means non or not, and nicca comes from the Sanskrit nitya, which means eternal, and therefore Anicca is understood to be not eternal, hence impermanence. Seeing this to be the case in one's own life through the experience of death, grief, heartbreak, illness, and unexpected disasters and situations, one sees the inherent transient nature of all that arises in one's life. This happens on a much deeper level through reflection born of samādhi, which is not initiated with trying, but just seeing and observing. And what is one observing? The very nature of the fabric of existence – that is to say, one is seeing the arising and passing away of elemental structures that can be categorized into various ways like the five aggregates. One can just notice how the experience of the senses is always changing, never stationary in any given moment, along with one's cognition tied to that experience. One observes at the deepest level the arising of the nidanas or links of Dependent Origination. This happens after deep virāga is established. When one sees this one realizes how quickly the links arose and passed away without one's own control or involvement in the process.

When one sees this quick flux-like nature of the cognitive building blocks of reality, one sees the fundamental Dukkha present, in that there is no link worth holding onto because it is inherently unstable by the very nature of its impermanence and therefore is not to be considered oneself because a core self would ideally be permanent and also sukha or that which is the nature of happiness – this is the key of Anatta, which is the understanding that there is a lack of a central and eternal homunculus controlling the processes. This knowledge gives rise to complete letting go and can occur in the total cementing of wisdom, liberating the mind from the deep-seated patterns of activity that are the Āsavas, and thus the completion of the Path and final knowledge that embeds the Four Noble Truths, making them visible here and now in every second.

The Three Views on Dukkha

There are three overarching views on Dukkha. The first two are broad categories under which similar theories and standpoints can be associated.

The first view is a view of the eternalist. The second view is that of annihilationism. The third view is the middle way, which brings forth the understanding of Dependent Origination.

One who possesses an eternalist view understands that Dukkha arises in this world, in this lifetime that is present. Based on this broad view, one considers oneself to be eternal one way or another, and that this world itself is one of Dukkha, yet there is a hereafter, an eternal plane where one's true nature of an immortal self will live out without any Dukkha whatsoever, in total peace, contentment, and harmony. From here stem various codes of beliefs in a heaven that will provide everything that one ever wanted and that it will be everlasting. However, the truth of the matter is that even the heavenly realms have a tinge of Dukkha.

Consider the idea of this eternal self that abides forever in this realm. Things tire out eventually. One gets bored after time. The same qualities of satisfaction and contentment can eventually lead to boredom and dullness. There is still craving present in this level of existence and there is still ignorance and conceit that continues to color the perception of this heavenly world in a way that causes Dukkha, even if it might be subtle and progressively perceivable over vast swathes of time. The fact that such a realm would exist forever could drive such a mind into delusion and even madness at a certain breaking point. On the flipside, the fact that such heavenly realms are impermanent presents the inherent Dukkha in them. No matter what enjoyments may be available in such realms, after many eons they will fade away.

The idea of an eternal hell itself is also mind-boggling. While this may initially motivate one towards good deeds and thoughts, such thoughts are from an intention rooted in aversion and holding onto the concept of an eternal self. This causes the mind to gravitate towards other wrong views, including associating the idea of permanent self to one or more of the five aggregates in different ways, leading to self-centric actions that can include motivations of craving, aversion, deceit, ignorance, and delusion. Therefore, such fear of an eternal hell being the grounds for good behavior can only last for so long because there are still present the wrong notions of self that are in the mind as well the notion of eternal Dukkha.

The second broad categories of view that have to do with annihilationism include the idea that self is tied to the life here and now and after that there is no Dukkha. Dukkha, in this view, is tied to the body, to the mind, to the experiences of the senses and so on, but after the dissolution of the body, there is no life hereafter, which means there is no Dukkha after death. With this view, one indulges the senses, squeezes the enjoyment of every moment with the idea that there is only a self that is tied to them and so while one acknowledges Dukkha, one only sees it tied to this life. One runs away from Dukkha through attachment to sensory experiences and in the process that attachment leads to committing unwholesome thoughts, speech and actions, developing into the eventual inclination at death that causes either heavy remorse or strong craving, projecting those desires into a new rebirth that is filled with Dukkha. A dangerous effect of this view is the misguided logic that if Dukkha is tied to this self in this life, then it would be better to end life right there and then to prevent further Dukkha from arising. This is the view that incorporates the meaningless of life found in nihilism and philosophical pessimism.

The third understanding is that of the Dhamma. Here, one earnestly seeks a way out of Dukkha and this seeking can lead to an introduction to the Dhamma. From here, one starts to follow Magga or the Noble Eightfold Path, adhering mind to the mundane Right View that there is meaning in life, in generosity, in gratitude to one's parents and elders, that there is a life here and after, that there are those who understand this and have wisdom. One adheres one's intention to Right Intention, letting go of attachment to experiences, cultivating Metta (loving-kindness) and Karuna (compassion), and then follows the precepts by refraining from intentionally harming life, speaking falsehoods, taking what is not given, committing sexual misconduct, and taking intoxicants that numb attention and causes reckless behavior. This leads to more wholesome choices in one's lifestyle and workplace, as well as the ability to use Right Effort to let go of unwholesome states and replace them with wholesome states. This practice provides the tool for Right Mindfulness and for the further and deeper meditation practice of Right Collectedness. Thereafter, the mind becomes purified to the point of gaining insight into Dependent Origination, the three characteristics, and most importantly the Four Noble

Truths. Through this, one has completely understood Dukkha, abandoned the causes of Dukkha, and cultivated and the way leading to Nirodha, the cessation of Dukkha in this very life as well as eliminating the factors that could cause further rebirth in other conditioned planes of existence filled with inherent Dukkha.

Jarā Ageing

Katamā ca, bhikkhave, jarā?

Yā tesaṁ tesaṁ sattānaṁ tamhi tamhi sattanikāye jarā jīraṇatā khaṇḍiccaṁ pāliccaṁ valittacatā āyuno saṁhāni indriyānaṁ paripāko, ayaṁ vuccati, bhikkhave, jarā.

And what is ageing? In whatever beings, of whatever group of beings, there is ageing, decrepitude, broken teeth, grey hair, wrinkled skin, shrinking with age, decay of the sense-faculties, that, monks, is called ageing.

- **DN 22, Mahāsatipaṭṭhāna Sutta**

We will revisit Jāti, or rebirth, which deserves a greater deal of understanding on its own in the next chapter. Now, Jarā is the decay of the bodily experience through senescence. Here the decay happens over time, but it is a constant reminder that all things are indeed impermanent. Jarā has been translated as old age, ageing, decay, worn out or wearing out, and so on – and since the word can be applied not only to the body itself but to the ageing of the planet, the stars, the cosmos and all of Saṃsāra itself, it would be best for the purposes of understanding on a broader level to use the term decay.

Decay arises in the body deceptively under the guise of development. Once there is conception, the zygote begins to form creating the structures of the embryo in the womb. These cells die out but, in their wake, new cells arise. The embryo develops into the fetus and that fetus develops into the fully formed infant ready to be born. Throughout this process the perspective is that there is growth happening, but that growth's shadow is also decay, for when the child is born, there is already further decay happening. It may seem to be development as hairs on the head grow, as the body becomes larger, as the joints become fused, and so on and so forth, and this development seems to continue all the way until adulthood. Then, usually in one's thirties one experiences or seems to experience decay because it becomes visible. In truth, all throughout this time, trillions of cells have decayed and died, giving rise to new cells all throughout the body, and so death follows and occurs in the body at the minutest levels even before what is formally the departure of vitality (ayu) and heat (usmā) from the body that is the final death of a single lifetime after which the cycle starts over again.

Decay of the Body

The process of decay is perceived and felt when one notices that the eyes don't seem to work as well anymore or they feel more strained than before, when one loses the ability to hear certain frequencies one could have just five years ago or a decade ago, when food doesn't seem to provide the same intensity of taste as before, when the body feels feeble as joints hurt from certain movements and muscles pull with stretches one could do easily just a few years before and digestion isn't as efficient as before, or when the mind seems to become forgetful more often and it takes longer to process certain information and there is more effort to concentrate or make decisions. These are all signs of decay of the sense faculties. When the skin starts to become looser and hair starts to fall out and become gray, when teeth fall out and bones seem to be weaker, or when there seems to be less energy to do the things one liked doing in the past, these are signs of decay through the ageing of the body.

In today's modern science, people are living longer and, in their later years, are able to live in comfort and with more energy. From a purely superficial perspective, anti-wrinkling creams, hair dyes, and fibers to hide bald spots, or hair transplants, plastic surgeries and other kinds of invasive procedures seemingly delay if not stop the ageing process in its tracks. But these are all artificial bandages used taped over a deep-rooted problem. Vitamins, supplements, superfoods and the like seem to provide nutritional advantages to be able to function at better if not optimal levels of health and energy, yet at the level of the chromosomes ageing is unavoidable. One can do everything to delay it with every method, diet, routine, and trend, but genomic structures are not positively affected.

Ayu Saṅkhāra and Telomeres

The telomeres that are the endcaps of the chromosomes are biological doomsday timers that determine the health, function, and ultimate demise of the body. Billionaires and large-scale corporations are throwing money into research to find out how to reverse the ageing process by revitalizing and rebuilding the already shorn telomeres. Yet, there hasn't been any success. The telomeres get shorter with each passing replication of cells and thus important information is lost or distorted through each process of replication, causing cellular mutations, which means that certain abilities to function optimally at the bodily level also diminish each time. Simply put, this translates into decay that is perceived and felt at the level of pain, organ dysfunction and other symptoms of ageing.

These shortening of these telomeres are determined by the ayu saṅkhāra or formations determining longevity, which are dependent upon the lifestyle choices one makes and the habits one form in the way of health. Incidentally, researchers have investigated on how loving-kindness meditation delays the shortening of telomeres, which was not the original intention at all with such meditation. Now all of this research as well as different methods that people use to try to defy the nature of decay is symptomatic of a mindset filled with craving and aversion, conceit and ignorance. In short, there is an identification with body whenever there is fear of bodily decay and death. It's one thing to treat an age-related illness, in which case one is taking care of the body through compassion and understanding, but it's another thing to get upset about superficial signs or even implicit symptoms of ageing, thus causing oneself further Dukkha.

Decay of Nature

There are other ways in which decay occurs beyond the body itself. Observing nature, one sees how leaves fall during certain times and how flowers decay. The planet itself is always in flux and is decaying at different levels, with lots of activity from its inhabitants being a cause, but even out in the cosmos, the sun slowly but surely is burning out. Even broader, galaxies contain stars that explode or implode, rupturing galactic structures and ultimately turning into black holes. The universe itself decays during periods when planets, stars, and galaxies wink out and life is extinguished on an incalculable scale of time and space. In other words, all things arising from causes and conditions, from the levels of the proton and below to the cells of all life to the gigantic cosmic bodies of the universe and beyond, will pass away, and that journey between these two points is Jarā.

Understanding Decay with Right Effort

Accepting and seeing decay as a natural part of life immediately brings relief to the mind. Seeing it with wisdom – that is understanding decay as impersonal makes it something not worth holding to or caring about – one becomes free of the mental pain born from unwise reflection on the process of decay. The unwise process is to take thoughts and ideas that cause one to identify with the body and feel bad about the process of ageing. Looking in the mirror and seeing a few wrinkles with unwise attention, which is without mindfulness of the three characteristics or Attention Rooted in Reality, will certainly bring about further craving and lead to further Dukkha. Seeing a bald spot and immediately feeling insecure about it, because one identifies with the body, is born from ignorance and conceit. Developing insecurities about one's age, whatever their signs may be, is a form of the First Noble Truth of Dukkha. When the mind becomes agitated by these signs and thinks about what could happen as a result or experience nostalgia towards one's youth or glory days, this is the Second Noble Truth of Taṇhā (craving). Letting go through Right Effort is the development of the Fourth Noble Truth of Magga (the Noble Eightfold Path) and experience a mind free of such thoughts is the Third Noble Truth of Nirodha (cessation of Dukkha).

Whenever craving, ignorance and conceit attached to reactions towards the natural process of ageing arise, one lets go through Right Effort, or the 6Rs. One

- Recognizes there is a thought attached to seeing decay that causes discomfort and aversion – this is Dukkha
- Releases the attention to that thought and brings that attention to the next step

- Relaxes any tension in mind and/or body, which is associated with the aversion, thus letting go of Tanhaa and experiencing Nirodha
- Re-smiles to uplift the mind
- Returns to a balanced mind that is content and non-attached, deepening Nirodha
- Repeats whenever mind drifts from the balanced mind and cultivating Magga

Byādhi

...byādhipi dukkho...

...illness is suffering...

- SN 56.11, Dhammacakkappavattana Sutta

There are different types of illnesses that one may suffer. These include but are not limited to infectious diseases, illnesses by malnutrition, hereditary diseases and physiological diseases. Some illnesses are preventable, and some are unpreventable. Some illnesses are acute, and some are chronic. Others are caused by lifestyle choices and others are due to certain deficiencies or imbalances. There are mental illnesses which can arise through various causes and conditions. Whatever the illness is, it will always cause some form of dis-ease, or discomfort or unease in mind or body or both, and thus all illnesses are Dukkha.

Health is a form of wealth and sukha. There are many beings who have wealth in the form of money and possessions, wonderful relationships, a good reputation, and so on, but all of those forms of wealth can be impinged by an illness. Illness causes trouble in the body and by extension one feels unhappy, unable to function as one would in an optimal way, and one's entire mindset is plagued by the effect of this illness. This can cause one to make rash decisions or see people in a different light and create unruly situations due to misunderstandings. Depending on the intensity of the illness, one can lose one's ability to enjoy life fully, because the illness can become the central focus in one's life, causing one to never completely be happy or present. Even if one were present, the nagging pain or distress caused by the illness colors that mindfulness. In the spirit of fully understanding Dukkha, let's take a look at some of the types of diseases afflicting the human condition at one point or another in time.

Infections

Infectious diseases are communicable illnesses born from pathogens such as viruses and bacteria and can penetrate the immunity wall of a being. These diseases can manifest various types of aches, pains, and other disorders within the organs of the body, such as respiratory discomfort and dysfunction, cardiac arrest, or even complete death if not treated. The common cold is an infectious illness arising from the rhinovirus, which continues to mutate and has multiple variations throughout the year. It is just a fact and symptom of life that at some point or another this common cold will affect the body, and it brings with it fever, congestion, stuffiness, malaise, weakness, and other symptoms. For about three to ten days, one suffers through this period of the common cold.

Other infectious illnesses can arise through various transmissions of viruses, bacteria, protozoa, and fungi. In this way, one can experience airborne transmission of viral droplets, foodborne transmission that can cause severe food poisoning and gastrointestinal pain, sexual transmission affecting the genitals primarily but can then affect other parts of the immune system as well as the organs of the body, intravenous transmission through needles, vector transmission such as through mosquitos who can carry for example malarial infections and the west Nile virus, waterborne transmission, skin transmission that can cause fungal infections like ringworm and athlete's foot, and transmission from the mother to the infant where the mother may have an existing infection which then transmits into the fetus thus causing the infant a pre-existing infection. All such infections can create varying degrees of unease, from a subtle but noticeable discomfort in the body to excruciating pain and even loss of life. Some infections may even lie dormant in the body and flare up intermittently during one's lifetime.

Malnutrition

Malnutrition is the severe lack of proper and efficient nutrification of the body. It can happen for those who have a lack of nutrients and thus face the wasting away of the body, while for others who may be overweight or even normal weight the body is unable to process certain nutrients effectively, thus causing imbalances as well as deficiencies of essential vitamins, minerals and other micronutrients. In the case of the malnourished due to lack of resources, there are several symptoms that be easily noticeable, such as a distended abdomen, skeletal frame, dry eyes, dry skin, muscular wasting, loose skin, and brittle or sparse hair among others. There are also internal symptoms such as slow heartrate, poor memory, delayed growth, skeletal deformities, loss of reflexes, as well as behavioral effects such as diminished cognitive capacities, lethargy, and anxiety.

In the case of nutritional deficiencies, the body can undergo large amounts of physical changes, such as kwashiorkor and marasmus due to protein and energy deficiencies respectively, osteoporosis and rickets due to calcium and vitamin D deficiency, goiter due to iodine deficiency, Keshan disease due to selenium deficiency, anemia due to iron deficiency, growth retardation due to zinc deficiency, beriberi due to thiamine deficiency, pellagra due to niacin deficiency, scurvy due to vitamin C deficiency, night blindness due to vitamin A deficiency and hemophilia due to vitamin K deficiency, among others.

On the other end of the spectrum, there is malnutrition in the form of over-nutrification of the body. This can include metabolic imbalances due to overeating, causing obesity, which can lead to other ailments like diabetes and cardiovascular issues. Then there is hypervitaminosis such as too much vitamin A that can cause all sorts of vision, appetite, bone, skin, and liver problems, or too much vitamin D that can cause large amounts calcium to be deposited in the bones, heart, tissues and kidneys causing dehydration, vomiting, fatigue and weakness, hypertension and cardiovascular disease. As a result of vitamin B3 toxicity, the body may suffer from liver inflammation, prediabetes, high levels of uric acid, macular swelling and cysts, and vitamin B6 toxicity can lead to peripheral neuropathy and other neurological and psychological issues. Too much iron can lead to liver failure, brain and other organ damage as well as shock, leading to potential death.

Genetic Disorders, NCDs, and Mental Illnesses

Genetic Disorders can be passed down from genes to another and can include physiological proclivity of the body towards certain conditions like a defective heart valve or other congenital heart conditions, Down Syndrome, cystic fibrosis, sickle cell disease, Huntington's disease, and can include other physiological illnesses like hypertension, Alzheimer's, cancer and even obesity. Genes play a major role in the way saṅkhārās arise and being carriers of kamma from one life to the next, this can include the diseases and defects the body may have a tendency to develop based on factors including but not limited to lifestyle choices, the strength of certain kamma, and even the environmental factors a being is subject to during their lifetime. Choices and intervention through corrective surgeries and even medications can help prevent the tendencies of awakening certain illnesses carried forward by genes as well treat pre-existing conditions.

NCDs, or non-communicable diseases, include problems with certain organs and bodily systems. This can include cardiovascular and cerebrovascular issues, diabetes, kidney disease, cancer, autoimmune disorders and chronic respiratory diseases. Vascular diseases can include strokes, heart failure, aneurysms, and vascular dementia among a whole host of other diseases. Diabetes can be type 1 where the pancreas loses its ability to produce insulin, due to the loss of certain cells as an autoimmune response, type 2 where gradual insulin resistance can lead to a lack of insulin for the body and this can be caused by lack of exercise and excessive bodyweight, or gestational where a pregnant woman develops high blood sugar levels. Kidney disease is where the kidney loses its ability to function, and it can be either acute or chronic in nature. Cancer is the overgrowth of cells, which fail to die, and this can cause damage to the body leading to malignant tumors and cysts, and it can happen in any one part of the body and spread if it becomes metastatic. Autoimmune disorders arise when the immune system attacks the body itself and this can lead to various types of disorders including diabetes, multiple sclerosis, lupus and over eighty different types of autoimmune disease. They can have genetic or environmental causes. Finally chronic respiratory illnesses include asthma and COPD are treatable but not yet curable.

Mental illnesses have a wide array of causes, ranging from genetic to environmental to autoimmune disorder to brain damage, which can happen while in the womb or external factors after one's birth. Substance abuse as well as infections and toxins can cause mental disorders, along with disorder in the neurotransmitter systems of the brain. Mental illnesses can include but are not limited to various types of anxiety and depression, bipolar disorder, schizophrenia, autism spectrum disorders, dementia, paranoia and psychosis.

Understanding Illness with Right Effort

Whatever the illness may be what one must see is that all illnesses arise out of causes and conditions. These causes and conditions are impermanent and impersonal and so when one sees the symptom of an illness arise, the first response to it should be to understand it as being indeed painful but not let the mind grasp onto it as self. Instead, the wise mind sees the impersonal nature of the illness and out of self-compassion, if possible, treats it with medicine and other procedures. The key is not just observing and forbearing the illness at the cost of not alleviating it but actually alleviating it in dual ways – first with the correct form of healing that may be available and second uprooting any mental attachments or aversions or identification towards the illness. Whenever there is pain from illness or thoughts related to that pain of the illness or anything related to the illnesses, this is the First Noble Truth of Dukkha. Whenever the mind wanders around further proliferates different viewpoints, scenarios, and ruminates, this is a form of the Second Noble Truth of Taṇhā. When the mind utilizes the 6Rs, one develops the Fourth Noble Truth of Magga and then experiences relief from the wandering mind, which is the Third Noble Truth of Nirodha.

When thoughts arise due to identifying with the body and one's anxieties are triggered by what-if scenarios after a diagnosis or one feels unwell physically or one's convalescence that deters one's mental peace, then one utilizes the 6Rs and

- Recognizes the anxiety, the depression, the worry, the anger, the sadness or whatever unwholesome state arising due to the pain or diagnosis of the illness or the discomfort that may initially arise as one starts to heal from an illness or is bedridden for the sake of healing – this is the First Noble Truth of Dukkha
- Releases their attention away from these unwholesome states of mind and brings them to the next step
- Relaxes any tension in mind and/or body associated with the unwholesome state – this is letting go of the Second Noble

Truth of Taṇhā and experiencing the Third Noble Truth of Nirodha

- Re-smiles to uplift the mind and deep the quietude of mind

- Returns to a more wholesome state of mind, if that means joy, tranquility, or just a balanced mind – this is the further deepening of the Third Noble Truth of Nirodha

- Repeats whenever mind becomes agitated again thus following the Fourth Noble Truth of Magga

Maraṇa Death

Katamañca, bhikkhave, maraṇaṁ? Yaṁ tesaṁ tesaṁ sattānaṁ tamhā tamhā sattanikāyā cuti cavanatā bhedo antaradhānaṁ maccu maraṇaṁ kālakiriyā khandhānaṁ bhedo kaḷevarassa nikkhepo jīvitindriyassupacchedo, idaṁ vuccati, bhikkhave, maraṇaṁ.

And what is death? In whatever beings, of whatever group of beings, there is a passing-away, a removal, a cutting-off, a disappearance, a death, a dying, an ending, a cutting-off of the aggregates, a discarding of the body, that, monks, is called death.

- DN 22, Mahāsatipaṭṭhāna Sutta

If you're reading this, you are going to die. When you were born, you came with an expiry date. That is the truth of existence. All who come into being will pass away. This one understanding, seeing it with purity of mind and complete equanimity brings about a profound realization, which comes in the form of opening the Dhammacakka, or the eye of the Dhamma and the perspective – "All that is subject to arising is to subject to passing away." Maraṇa is this passing away. It is inevitable, no matter what dimension of existence you are currently occupying, whether it's the realms of hell, the animal world, the human world, the higher octaves of dimensions of the devas or brahmas or the pure realms of anāgāmis and arahants who have become so in those pure realms or even the formless realms – all dimensions are conditioned, brought about by a series of causes, and some of these unravel into destruction, or an end of existing in them. Maraṇa can mean dissolution, death, ending, destruction and so on, and so these words can be used interchangeably. This unraveling process from Jāti to Jarā to Maraṇa is kamma (the Pali for the Sanskrit karma), which is a series of activities that are compounded by various causes and conditions, manipulated and made to an end or brought to further unraveling by intention and choice in every moment.

The Certitude of Death

Now the only way out of Maraṇa is to enter the amata, the deathless, which is another term for Nibbāna (Nirvāna in Sanskrit). It is called thus because in Nibbāna, there is no birth and therefore no death can follow. Nibbāna as a word is made elusive by various concepts. The irony is the mind wants to understand Nibbāna rather than actually experience it. There is a subtle difference between understanding and experiencing. One may understand the taste of sugar by having read and heard about it, but one truly experiences when the sugar touches the tastebuds, at which point there is full comprehension. To experience is to fully understand, but to understand by mere concepts is not to experience. In the same way, how can one fully experience something that is non-conceptual with the use of concepts? One can certainly understand something this way, and this knowledge will aid in the experience by recognizing what something is and isn't – the same can be said of Maraṇa. It may be that one may say one has never experienced death and even if one certainly experienced dissolution in a previous life one may not recall this event.

Death surrounds us. Our cells experience decay and ultimately die and yet there is no notice of this activity. Death always remains with us in the form of the death of our loved ones, of plants and animals, and in the form of the destruction of things we have produced or created like music, literature, art, or buildings or cities or large civilizations and empires. All have come to an end. We've seen it and learned about it. Therefore, by seeing it, and hearing and learning about it, we understand the concept of death.

We continue to hear about the death of beings on the news but because of the distancing of such an event from our lives, the mindset is so numbed to it that at one end it accepts death but only peripherally and on the other becomes completely flustered to the point of debilitating anxiety and depression when it happens to someone close to us. The exposure to violence and the many incidents of war over one's lifetime have desensitized the mind to death to the point that it has a certain apathetic nature towards death and the dying, void of compassion and understanding. Beings live in such a way as if they will live forever even when death surrounds them. Even the devas and Brahmas, having long lifespans amounting to billions and even trillions of years, will all end. Even though their timescale differs from that of human reckoning, they still live for such long periods that they more often than not forget that they are actually mortal and start to invest in the false belief of an immortal self and eternal heaven in which they reside.

In a human lifetime, death follows birth. It can happen in any which way depending on one's kamma, both that which one inherits from previous lifetimes as well from the choices one makes in every moment. The key is to understand this before one regrets this fact. On the deathbed of one uninstructed in the Dhamma, the mind is fraught with all sorts of emotions, thoughts, and memories. Depending upon the inclination of the mind during that life, various beliefs can form, including the view of the eternalist, in which case one may have delight in going to an eternal heaven or fear of going to an eternal hell. If one is of the annihilationist view, then one may still have regrets that one wasn't able to fully live the life they wanted or may delight in the notion that Dukkha is finally over with the passing of this life's last breath. In all cases, such thoughts present in mind will lead to further rebirth that continues to lead to further death since these thoughts are fettered by craving and hindered by ignorance.

If one instead understood death as being conditioned as well, as being Dukkha, and turns the mind away from craving and abandons attachments or aversions, this can lead in the best-case full awakening or in the worst-case stream entry. If one understands that there is no personal nature to any of the five aggregates, then there is no clinging possible for a future renewal of being to occur. Instead, those five aggregates will dissolve with no new consciousness to evolve into a new rebirth.

We will explore this in much greater detail at a later point in time, but for now one should contemplate what death means to the mind at the moment. Does it bring fear, or does it bring acceptance through wisdom? Death is but another unraveling that is kamma and one must face it at some point or another, so understand it to be an unavoidable form of Dukkha that even the Buddha faced with total understanding and perfect wisdom.

The Seven Suns

Aniccā, bhikkhave, saṅkhārā; adhuvā, bhikkhave, saṅkhārā, anassāsikā, bhikkhave, saṅkhārā. Yāvañcidaṁ, bhikkhave, alameva sabbasaṅkhāresu nibbindituṁ alaṁ virajjituṁ alaṁ vimuccituṁ.

Bhikkhus, conditioned phenomena are impermanent; conditioned phenomena are unstable; conditioned phenomena are unreliable. It is enough to become disenchanted with all conditioned phenomena, enough to become dispassionate toward them, enough to be liberated from them.

- AN 7.66, Sattasūriya Sutta

The planet Earth is impermanent. On its surface and within its waters and many underground tunnels and caverns, many beings have lived and survived, but over billions of years, all kinds of beings have arisen and passed away. From proto-bacteria to more sentient beings like the first water-dwellers to the dinosaurs and to the humans, Earth has witnessed the rise and fall of many species and dominant beings. Humanity, as we know it today, is but a few minutes old if the planet's history was on a clock. Humanity will die out, one way or another, and the planet will still be here. However, that will not always be the case. There will be phases of destruction that even the planet that has been around for billions of years will face over the next few billion years through a series of growth spurts from the sun. The Buddha explained this process in the Sattasūriya Sutta, where he described seven distinct phases in time concerning the sun's evolution and how it affects the planet humans call home as just an iota of cosmic dust. In doing so, the Buddha indicated that even the greater aspects of the cosmos go through destruction and are not immune to the impermanent nature of reality. Like all conditioned things, the planets, stars, and galaxies are impermanent, and there is Dukkha in all of them, and none of them can be taken personally.

In the first phase, the sun grows hotter than we may understand it during humanity's time, so hot that it will destroy vegetation, plants, and seed life. This results in the decay and eventual demise of all beings who subsist on vegetation for their sustenance. Most beings at this point will be destroyed by the increase of blazing radiation from the sun which will also destroy the possibility of any sustainable atmosphere and of a stable and predictable rain cycle.

In the second to fifth phases, there is the gradual decay of more life as freshwater sources begin to evaporate and the life in them dies off. Then the larger lakes start to dry up and most small animals are driven underground or to the poles. All large animals at this point will be completely extinct. Small insects, microbes, certain birds, and others may survive based on their instincts, some small animals venturing into the caverns of the Earth and others shifting to the poles where it will be cooler and possibly more sustainable. However, the oceans too will dry up, and much before then, all but a very few, such as single-cell organisms, will be around, but eventually, they too will die off.

In the sixth stage, the Earth becomes intensely hot, even for the smallest microbes to survive. At this point, it becomes one giant planet of hell – with fuming volcanoes and landscapes of flowing lava in every part. Life has completely evaporated. Nothing, not even halophiles who subsist on areas of highly concentrated salt or any atmospheric beings, will survive this phase. At the final stage, the Earth's gravitational field is heavily manipulated, and the orbit of the moon will no longer remain steady. The sun becomes a red giant and engulfs the Earth and moon. The planet becomes a flaming ball before disintegrating into its final end, leaving nothing in its wake.

Three Types of Cosmic Destruction

There comes a time after many eons, many billions of years, when a cosmic destruction occurs that eradicates all forms. This can happen seven times through fire and at the eighth time through water. After a succession of eight cycles of seven fiery destructions and a watery destruction, there is a cosmic destruction by wind. Then this cycle repeats again through the eons of decay and destruction. Depending upon the destruction, not just the human and lower realms but even the higher realms of devas, brahmas and mahabrahmas are destroyed with the exception of the Vehapphala devas and above.

The destruction by fire arises when the thousand world systems – that is to say, a cluster of galaxies – ignite due to many stellar explosions and other kind of radiation and fiery bursts. The heat of these intense behemoths annihilates the structures of the lower realms, inflames and disintegrates the various worlds on which humans are born, and obliterates the subtle luminous structures of the higher worlds, including of the devas and the brahmas but not the Ābhassara realms or beyond. Such a destruction can radiate out for many millions of light years throughout and all lifeforms are instantly destroyed. However, in their wake nebula of gas arise and start to form new material that then recreates new planets and suns upon the start of a new eon. After many billions of years, beings inhabiting the Ābhassara realms go down to the realms of the brahmas and mahabrahmas and then to the human realms and the process of kamma initiates activity in the lower realms as well when these proto-humans start to build up coarse craving.

Destruction by water is something entirely different. It is understood that the world rests on water, but we must understand this from another perspective. In the literal sense, yes, there is a whole other ocean under the Earth's mantle, and there is a possibility of the planet's destruction by a quake large enough to cause this ocean to destroy the planet inside out. However, the destruction of water is widespread. The water element refers not only to the water as humans understand it but also to the quality of a substance being cohesive or sticky and wave-like. This cohesive, sticky, and wave-like quality is best understood in the form of gravity, which holds things in place, from the sun to the planets to their moons and so on. When a destruction by water occurs, it happens when there is a massive disturbance of gravity. In this case, a super massive black hole can devour entire galaxies creating widescale destruction. This destruction can affect a supercluster of galaxies and an area of hundreds of millions of light years. When this happens, the Ābhassara realms are also destroyed, and only the beings of the Subhakiṇṇa realms and beyond survive since the destruction's height scales all the way up to that limit. Later, when there is a renewal of being in another eon, the Subhakiṇṇa beings descend down to the Ābhassara and so on, until their kamma repopulates the human realms and lower realms.

Finally, there is the cosmic destruction by wind. One can call this the gravitational field, dark energy or dark matter but whatever one wants to call it, it is due to the contraction of the fabric of the universe itself which is exerted in the form of a cosmic wind. It affects the entire span of the universe itself and rips away the structures of realms all the way up to the Vehapphala realms. At another eon of repopulation and the renewal of creation of lower realms, the kamma of beings here will run out and they will take birth in lower realms all the way down to the hell realms when in the human realms there are beings who commit unwholesome activities.

There is Dukkha inherent in the cosmos by the very fact that they are subject to destruction, built up by causes and conditions that can pass away through any of the abovementioned processes. Death is inescapable even at the level of the galaxies, and therefore one must see that if this is the case, death on the human scale is but an almost imperceivable twinkle compared to the cosmic displays of fiery, watery, and windy destructions.

Understanding Death with Right Effort

What's important to understand is that while death and the Dukkha experienced in the form of this process is unavoidable, whether being experienced firsthand or exposed to it by the death of another, there are ways to accept this with wisdom and understanding and to use the 6Rs to let go of the aversions and hindrances arising from such events. When you face death, it is the First Noble Truth of Dukkha. When you grasp onto that experience with a sense of "I am" or have craving or aversion towards the experience, it is the Second Noble Truth of Taṇhā. When you use the 6Rs, you are implementing the Fourth Noble of the Path, and when you experience the relief from having let go of the Second Noble Truth of Taṇhā, you experience the Third Noble Truth of Nirodha.

Let's say you find out your friend, loved one, relative, or a family member has passed away. The first reactions to that Dukkha will be painful, pleasant, or neutral. If it's someone who was close to you and you had a strong attachment to them, there can arise painful feelings associated with their passing away. If it was someone you didn't like and perhaps harbored hatred for, there might be a pleasant feeling. If it was someone you didn't have an interest in or think about or didn't know, anxieties could arise out of your own reflection of death, or you may just think that they died, and one day you will too, but there is a subtle identification arising here. This subtle identification arises due to ignorance born from a lack of mindfulness and allowing the mind to wander around with thoughts of a personal self in some manner or another. For example, you hear about the death of a famous person, and you don't give too much heed to it, but you use that as a way to discuss or to be the first one to tell someone about the news. There's a sense of personal gain for the "I" present. Whatever the case may be, here is how one can implement the 6Rs to let go of the Dukkha of death as a witness to it.

- Recognize when mind starts to drift into anxieties, grief, sadness at the news of the demise of a loved one, or starts to get relieved by the news of someone one hates, or personalize a neutral response for the "self's" gain
- Release attention to these wandering thoughts and bring it to the next step
- Relax the tension and let go of any mental or physical grasping and feel the space of tranquility
- Re-smile to uplift the mind – even a small one makes a big difference
- Return to the tranquility of mind
- Repeat whenever mind begins to wander again

Seeing death can be a traumatic experience. It can leave a deep-rooted memory that can cause grief, pain, and mental imbalance. Grief is a natural response, but the key is to see how the mind reacts. The seeing of death of someone itself can cause shock to the system and later on, the body releases certain hormones that cause mind to get into a state of delirium or further shock, depending on the inclinations of a person. In SN 47.13, Cunda Sutta, the Venerable Ānanda found out about the Parinibbāna of the Venerable Sāriputta. He proclaimed to the Buddha that –

Api ca me, bhante, madhurakajāto viya kāyo, disāpi me na pakkhāyanti, dhammāpi maṁ nappaṭibhanti 'āyasmā sāriputto parinibbuto'ti sutvā

Venerable sir, since I heard that the Venerable Sāriputta has attained final Nibbāna, my body seems as if it has been drugged; I have become disoriented, and the teachings are no longer clear to me.

To which the Buddha replied

Kiṁ nu kho te, ānanda, sāriputto sīlakkhandhaṁ vā ādāya parinibbuto, samādhikkhandhaṁ vā ādāya parinibbuto, paññākkhandhaṁ vā ādāya parinibbuto, vimuttikkhandhaṁ vā ādāya parinibbuto, vimuttiñāṇadassanakkhandhaṁ vā ādāya parinibbuto"ti?

Why, Ānanda, when Sāriputta attained final Nibbāna, did he take away your aggregate of virtue, or your aggregate of concentration, or your aggregate of wisdom, or your aggregate of liberation, or your aggregate of the knowledge and vision of liberation?

Ānanda explains that the Venerable Sāriputta had been a great teacher who inspired him and gladdened him, providing him counsel in the teachings. The Buddha then says –

Nanu taṁ, ānanda, mayā paṭikacceva akkhātaṁ: 'sabbehi piyehi manāpehi nānābhāvo vinābhāvo aññathābhāvo.

But have I not already declared, Ānanda, that we must be parted, separated, and severed from all who are dear and agreeable to us?

And later in the sutta provides Ānanda with the oft-quoted admonishment –

Tasmātihānanda, attadīpā viharatha attasaraṇā anaññasaraṇā, dhammadīpā dhammasaraṇā anaññasaraṇā.

Therefore, Ānanda, dwell with yourselves as your own island, with yourselves as your own refuge, with no other refuge; dwell with the Dhamma as your island, with the Dhamma as your refuge, with no other refuge.

It may be that the event is so traumatic for one who sees death and whose mind is untrained – remember, even the non-liberated monastics who witnessed the Buddha's passing were overcome with painful emotions – that they are unable to come back to a more centered or balanced mind. If such is the case, then whenever one recovers, one should reflect and review and see whenever a painful mental feeling arises and then use the 6Rs to retrain the mind from wincing at his death.

- Recognize the mental feeling of grief and shock and how the mind drifts from being centered
- Release attention and bring it to mind and body
- Relax the tension between mind and body, thus alleviating any stress and letting go of the craving and aversion
- Re-smile to uplift the mind
- Return to a more wholesome state of the mind
- Repeat whenever mind drifts away again

What about when you are facing death? Consider the idea right now and see what kind of reactions the mind produces at the thought of its own demise. If there is a mental wince, pain in the mind that cringes at such a thought, or if there are any thoughts that arise out of the miseries of life, which is to say the mind relishes in the idea of death because it will be an end to Dukkha, both are symptoms of craving, and both are rooted in ignorance. At one end, the mind may feel horrified at the prospect of one's own death. There may be ideas of there's so much to accomplish before death or how will your friends and family feel after you are gone. Alternatively, the mind thinks about the sweet release of death as being final, and the extreme case of this would be having suicidal tendencies, which we will explore further and deeper in a little bit. Both are rooted in the idea of a personal self, which is what needs to be seen and let go of in order to attain pure wisdom.

There are two suggestions the Buddha provided to balance out the mind and understand death as a reality without causing further Dukkha. First, for one tied to the body, to one's possessions, to the idea of a self that is identified with the body, the Buddha recommended doing the contemplation on the stages of decay of a dead body –

- A corpse that is thrown aside in a charnel ground, one, two, or three days dead, bloated, livid, and oozing matter
- Being devoured by crows, hawks, vultures, dogs, jackals, or various kinds of worms,
- A skeleton with flesh and blood, held together with sinews
- A fleshless skeleton smeared with blood, held together with sinews
- A skeleton without flesh and blood, held together with sinews

- Disconnected bones scattered in all directions — here a hand-bone, there a foot-bone, here a shin-bone, there a thigh-bone, here a hip-bone, there a back-bone, here a rib-bone, there a breast-bone, here an arm-bone, there a shoulder-bone, here a neck-bone, there a jaw-bone, here a tooth, there the skull
- Bones bleached white, the color of shells, bones heaped up
- Bones more than a year old,
- Bones rotted and crumbled to dust

So imameva kāyaṁ upasaṁharati: "ayampi kho kāyo evaṁdhammo evaṁbhāvī evaṁanatīto'ti."

A bhikkhu compares this same body with it thus: "This body too is of the same nature, it will be like that, it is not exempt from that fate."

- MN 10, Satipaṭṭhāna Sutta

The Buddha also recommended the following to let go of the fear of death with a statement to reflect and contemplate deeply, allowing the mind to accept the truth of Maraṇa and understand the nature of Dukkha as a whole, by which one destroys the fetters tying one to Saṃsāra –

Na kho ahaññeveko maraṇadhammo maraṇaṁ anatīto, atha kho yāvatā sattānaṁ āgati gati cuti upapatti sabbe sattā maraṇadhammā maraṇaṁ anatītā'ti. Tassa taṁ ṭhānaṁ abhiṇhaṁ paccavekkhato maggo sañjāyati. So taṁ maggaṁ āsevati bhāveti bahulīkaroti. Tassa taṁ maggaṁ āsevato bhāvayato bahulīkaroto saṁyojanāni sabbaso pahīyanti, anusayā byantīhonti.

This noble disciple reflects thus: "I am not the only one who is subject to death, not exempt from death. All beings that come and go, pass away and undergo rebirth, are subject to death; none are exempt from death." As he often reflects on this theme, the path is generated. He pursues this path, develops it, and cultivates it. As he does so, the fetters are entirely abandoned, and the underlying tendencies are uprooted.

- AN 5.57, Abhiṇhapaccavekkhitabbaṭhāna Sutta

Suppose you have any regrets or remorse or attachments to beings, situations, and desires for achieving something before death - as you consider the prospect of your impending demise - in that case, they all stem from craving, conceit, and ignorance.

Such fuel will cause further renewal of being and rebirth. In the first case, it will cause Dukkha here and now and cause one to think, say or act in a way that causes further Dukkha, while in the second case, it will cause one to hold onto such thoughts on the deathbed, giving rise to a new rebirth in a new life. In either case, the cycle of Dukkha continues. Therefore, when you see this, you implement Right Effort –

- Recognize the First Noble Truth of Dukkha present in unpleasant feelings or grasping at the craving to achieve something before death or when such feelings arise during the process of death
- Release attention and put it on mind and body
- Relax mind and body and therefore abandon the Second Noble Truth of Taṇhā
- Re-smile to uplift the mind
- Return to the tranquil mind of having relaxed, thus experiencing the Third Noble Truth of Nirodha
- Repeat whenever mind becomes agitated, and by doing so, one continues to implement the Fourth Noble Truth of Magga

Sokaparidevadukkhadomanassupāyāsā

Katamo ca, bhikkhave, soko? Yo kho, bhikkhave, aññataraññatarena byasanena samannāgatassa aññataraññatarena dukkhadhammena phuṭṭhassa soko socanā socitattaṁ antosoko antoparisoko, ayaṁ vuccati, bhikkhave, soko.

And what is sorrow? Whenever, by any kind of misfortune, anyone is affected by something of a painful nature, sorrow, mourning, distress, inward grief, inward woe, that, monks, is called sorrow.

Katamo ca, bhikkhave, paridevo? Yo kho, bhikkhave, aññataraññatarena byasanena samannāgatassa aññataraññatarena dukkhadhammena phuṭṭhassa ādevo paridevo ādevanā paridevanā ādevitattaṁ paridevitattaṁ, ayaṁ vuccati, bhikkhave, paridevo.

And what is lamentation? Whenever, by any kind of misfortune, anyone is affected by something of a painful nature and there is crying out, lamenting, making much noise for grief, making great lamentation, that, monks, is called lamentation.

Katamañca, bhikkhave, dukkhaṁ? Yaṁ kho, bhikkhave, kāyikaṁ dukkhaṁ kāyikaṁ asātaṁ kāyasamphassajaṁ dukkhaṁ asātaṁ vedayitaṁ, idaṁ vuccati, bhikkhave, dukkhaṁ.

And what is pain? Whatever painful bodily feeling, unpleasant bodily feeling, painful or unpleasant feeling results from bodily contact, that, monks, is called pain.

Katamañca, bhikkhave, domanassaṁ? Yaṁ kho, bhikkhave, cetasikaṁ dukkhaṁ cetasikaṁ asātaṁ manosamphassajaṁ dukkhaṁ asātaṁ vedayitaṁ, idaṁ vuccati, bhikkhave, domanassaṁ.

And what is sadness? Whatever painful mental feeling, unpleasant mental feeling, painful or unpleasant sensation results from mental contact, that, monks, is called sadness.

Katamo ca, bhikkhave, upāyāso? Yo kho, bhikkhave, aññataraññatarena byasanena samannāgatassa aññataraññatarena dukkhadhammena phuṭṭhassa āyāso upāyāso āyāsitattaṁ upāyāsitattaṁ, ayaṁ vuccati, bhikkhave, upāyāso.

And what is distress? Whenever, by any kind of misfortune, anyone is affected by something of a painful nature, distress, great distress, affliction with distress, with great distress, that, monks, is called distress.

- DN 22, Mahāsatipaṭṭhāna Sutta

Sorrow and Lamentation

We touched upon sorrow in the form of grief earlier, but now let us explore what this sorrow, which includes the experience of grief, entails. Sorrow and lamentation are the mind's responses when something terrible happens. There can be a loss of a person, of one's possessions, or a great feeling of loss in general. The mind can shut down as a reaction and begin to loop together all sorts of unpleasant views, ideas, and imaginings that creates further Dukkha. Sorrow as a reaction to the loss of a person, whether by death or by choice – meaning the breaking up of a relationship, the drifting apart of one friend from another by long distances – or not by choice where the mentioned examples can happen due to unforeseen circumstances, which result in the separation of loved ones. War, famine, an arrest, disruption in society through revolts and even genocide can be sources of separation and misfortune. Consider the history of the German occupation during the Second World War, where people lived in fear or those who were persecuted and sent to concentration camps, never able to see their loved ones again. The displacement of an entire community of people, or refugees from war-torn countries, has seen the separation of children from their parents, or siblings from one another, or spouses from one another, not to mention the deaths that are suffered by victims and the grief experienced by their families in places where riots and insurrections arise.

The attachment the mind has towards a person becomes deeply ingrained from a young age, first towards one's parents or caretakers, then towards friends and lovers. The first time a child goes to school can be harrowing for both parents and the child, where for an extended amount of time, the child is away from their caretaker. For the first few hours, the child feels anxious and may even lament, wailing, and bawling, but in a little while, they start adapting to their new environment and even start to make new friends. As days go on, this attachment is projected onto friends. For parents, as adults, they may be able to cope by getting their mind distracted with work or other things to do for the day, but the absence of their child, if they're working from home, is in the background of their thoughts. Perhaps, they are more used to it when they have to go to work and know they will see their child again, and the child may have gotten used to this same sort of routine after understanding that their mother or father return home every evening, so they are assured of this conditioned truth in their mind. But this separation is new territory for the time being.

When a child is with their parents at the mall or store or supermarket, and they get enamored by something and start to walk away and then go back to look for their parents, they don't find them. Their attachment to the parent comes to the forefront of their mind, and they lament, thinking they've lost their parents, and what may seem like a few minutes appears to be hours, and all sorts of terrible thoughts infused with fear and grief arise and proliferate in the child's mind until there is relief when they see their parents once again. Likewise, the parents are fraught with worry and anxiety, desperately searching for their children until they find them and experience shedding of that worry. The pang of separation is intense, but the relief is equally uplifting. This push-pull syndrome in mind is the fetter of craving and aversion. It manifests as sorrow when there is a separation from the object of that craving in the untrained mind.

Deeper levels of sorrow are experienced as one progresses through life. Experiencing the death of a loved one is a massive shock. That death is a natural part of life. Understand the nature of such sorrow. Yes, there is sadness for the loss of someone but was it for that someone alone? In other words, when someone the mind is attached to dies, what goes away with the departed are all the expectations, hopes, dreams, the investment of emotion, and pleasant feelings associated with them. When someone is in grief or sorrow at the death of a loved one, this line of thinking manifests with statements like, "How will I continue living without them," "We had so many things planned, but now that's all gone," "I wish I could tell them how much I loved them one last time," and so on. Essentially, the source of that sorrow is the attachment to the desires and identification projected onto the departed. Now that they're gone, there's no way for the mind to fulfill its desires since they were dependent upon them being alive. Likewise, at the ending of a relationship, as with the death of someone, there are nostalgic thoughts of the "good old days" and a feeling of sorrow at the impossibility of reliving those times, and there is sadness for what could have been had the relationship or the person continued on – this is another symptom of that same craving – and the lashing out, the lamentation, the wailing, and crying are manifestations of the mind that says, "I don't like and I don't want this to happen," i.e. aversion. This same pattern of thought can arise towards the loss of one's home and possessions as well as to the loss of an ideal such as innocence or one's livelihood.

There is the sorrow one may experience when one sees the suffering of others. Those whose minds may be more prone to emotion and have greater sensitivity can also experience sorrow when they see or hear news or stories of people dying from hunger or the torture of animals or the beings suffering through war and oppression, disease and pain and strife. This sadness can sometimes manifest as anger and more afflictive emotions, which will discuss further when we explore sadness and distress. One has to observe this sorrow first and understand it to be arising from identifying with these stories.

Here, sympathy or deep empathy can arise, but this causes the mind to take the pain of these beings as one's own, thus debilitating one's ability to function in a way that can provide meaningful change in those being's circumstances if one was inclined to do something about it. One must see this and turn this pity into compassion. Pity causes one to continue to proliferate identification with the situation. Compassion is when one understands the suffering present but doesn't involve the mind through identification. Compassion brings about understanding and an effective plan of action of how best to alleviate the suffering is possible and this is rooted in Right Intention and so whatever action may be taken with be done through the Noble Eightfold Path. If nothing can be done, sending out the feeling of compassion to those beings in suffering will cause the mind to relax and become tranquil.

Understanding Sorrow and Lamentation with Right Effort

One examines the sorrow with mindfulness, which provides the mind the ability to let go of the sorrow. Lamentation is a vocal manifestation of that sorrow. Noticing this, one sees that the First Noble Truth of Dukkha has arisen through this process of sorrow and lamentation. Whenever one witnesses the self-proliferation of nostalgia or mentally going through scenarios that can never be experienced due to the loss of a person or a possession, one abandons these flurries of emotions that make up the Second Noble Truth of Taṇhā. Having done so, one fulfills the Fourth Noble Truth of Magga by having implemented Right Effort or the 6Rs and thus realizes the relief from having let go – that is the Third Noble Truth of Nirodha. And so, one

- Recognizes – notices when the mind is subjected to sorrow and proliferates thoughts of sorrow, as well as recognizes that when one is crying or lamenting, it is a result of this sorrow or the First Noble Truth of Dukkha
- Releases – directs the attention away from the craving in the form of thoughts of nostalgia, pity, self-pity, grief, and pondering what could have been, and moves that attention to the next step
- Relaxes – loosens up tension in the body and mind associated with the thoughts of sorrow or letting go of the

Second Noble Truth of Taṇhā and experiencing the Third Noble Truth of Nirodha

- Re-smiles – this is important to bring about an uplifted mind, which replaces the grief-stricken mind with thoughts of comfort and tranquility

- Returns – directs mind to the sense of balance and equanimity, where mind is free of sorrow or experiencing the deepening of the Third Noble Truth of Nirodha

- Repeats – whenever mind drifts back to the sorrow, the pity, or the mental pain, one reiterates the process again, each time letting go of sorrow further and replacing it with more wisdom, which is utilizing the Fourth Noble Truth of Magga

Pain

Sutavā ca kho, bhikkhave, ariyasāvako dukkhāya vedanāya phuṭṭho samāno na socati, na kilamati, na paridevati, na urattāḷiṁ kandati, na sammohaṁ āpajjati. So ekaṁ vedanaṁ vedayati— kāyikaṁ, na cetasikaṁ. Seyyathāpi, bhikkhave, purisaṁ sallena vijjheyya. Tamenaṁ dutiyena sallena anuvedhaṁ na vijjheyya. Evañhi so, bhikkhave, puriso ekasallena vedanaṁ vedayati.

"Bhikkhus, when the instructed noble disciple is contacted by a painful feeling, he does not sorrow, grieve, or lament; he does not weep beating his breast and become distraught. He feels one feeling—a bodily one, not a mental one. Suppose they were to strike a man with a dart, but they would not strike him immediately afterwards with a second dart, so that the man would feel a feeling caused by one dart only.

- SN 36.6, Salla Sutta

The imagery of the dart, or an arrow, as a painful feeling is a perfect way to understand how there are two types of responses to the same painful feeling. In the Salla Sutta, the Buddha explains that the untrained mind experiences two feelings even though it experiences only one feeling of pain. That is to say, for the untrained mind when there arises a painful feeling, like a stomach cramp, muscle pull, or when one stubs their pinky toe, the immediate reaction is to project onto it the physical feeling a mental painful feeling filled with aversion and identification. Aversion here would be self-judgment, worry, anxiety, even anger at oneself for the physical painful feeling. Identification would be where the painful feeling is taken to be personal where, one thinks, "my stomach pains therefore I am in pain," or "I stubbed my stupid toe; I'm such an idiot," and so on. This results in wanting the pain to stop and therefore ignites craving. These reactions are rooted in ignorance where one doesn't see the scope of the Four Noble Truths present in this experience.

In the case of one following the Noble Eightfold Path, they have mindfulness to see what happens in mind as a result of the physical painful feeling. Whatever the feeling may be, their attention is on letting go of any attachment, aversion, or identification to the pain. If the mind becomes contracted around the pain, the mind will forgive the pain and let it go, especially if there is a recoil of self-hatred to self-anger present and thus these are given the antidotes of loving-kindness to oneself and self-compassion. Pain can arise from multiple sources. If it's not caused by one's own lapse in awareness of one's surroundings, it can arise due to an accident cause by another, by injuries sustained by that accident, by assaults or contact with terrible weather – such as a searing hot day or icy cold conditions – or the pain from an illness.

Whatever the cause, one has to see it as what it actually is – Anicca, Dukkha, and Anatta. Pain is a result of previous causes and conditions, and it doesn't always remain in one uniform sensation, even if the pain is dull continuous. There are variations within that pain as well, and if one's attention is focused on it then it will only intensify, which means that pain is not the same pain it was at initial contact. In reality, this pain is a reflection of mind which takes the pain to be permanent and affecting the mind personally. Such pain then is actually millions of body consciousnesses in a second, each of which dies out as soon as they arise. How one takes this determines whether the mind then gives experiences further Dukkha or Nirodha in its place. That's to say, if the mind takes the pain to be self, then this rooted in ignorance, causing mind to identify with and personalize it, leading to aversion and delight when the pain subsides. Such delight is rooted in craving because it identifies with the relief as well.

Therefore, whenever the training mind perceives the pain, it must become aware of where mind is in relation to the pain and if there is present these fetters of ignorance, craving, and aversion, thus personalizing the experience, the mind has an intention of seeing them and letting them go by redirecting the attention away from the reaction, relaxing, uplifting the mindset, then bringing attention to a feeling of forgiveness or self-compassion if there is an expression of self-hatred or anger, or to a balanced mind that is tranquil, observing with wisdom and Attention Rooted in Reality. The more the mind witnesses this process with wisdom and applies the Path in this way, the more it will see reality as it is and eventually whenever a physical pain makes contact with the body, it will know it as painful but will not react with unwholesome states but respond accordingly, treating the pain if it can be treated, and seeing it as impermanent, not worth holding on to, and impersonal.

Understanding Pain with Right Effort

Pain is a physical process that arises when there in a physical unpleasant experience born from contact of the body with a painful stimulus. The stimulus can be anything and in fact it doesn't matter what the stimulus is because it is just an impersonal condition that conjoins with the body and body-consciousness to bring about the experience of pain. Therefore, none of this process is the problem to be solved once it has happened, meaning it's not the contact, the stimulus, the body, or the painful feeling that one needs to understand as the issue. To clarify, there is Dukkha present in the links of contact and feeling as well as the body itself and the stimulus because they are all conditions and conditioned, and they are all, therefore, Dukkha and impersonal. However, after the fact of the pain itself, what is the point in lamenting and having negative, unwholesome reactions to the impersonal causes themselves? At this point, it's those conditions that are the issue to understand and let go but the reaction itself, which can cause further Dukkha to arise.

What one has to be mindful of is the reaction and the quality of that reaction. It's the craving present in that reaction that must be let go of in order to bring back mind to a more wholesome state. Therefore, when a painful feeling arises, whether it occurs through an assault, accident, climate, illness, or any other condition, if mind takes it personal, gets upset by it, has a response that feeds into the craving, thus giving rise to further Dukkha, one recognizes that there is first present the pain in the form of the First Noble Truth of Dukkha as well as the secondary Dukkha that arose from the Second Noble Truth of Taṇhā – taking the process personal and reacting from a mindset of "I hate this," "I want this to stop," or "I am in pain." One notices this and utilizes the Fourth Noble Truth of Magga via the 6Rs and experiences the disappearance of that Dukkha that is the Third Noble Truth of Nirodha. Let's then see how one utilizes the process whenever any form of physical pain arises. One

- Recognizes that mind grasps onto a painful feeling with afflictive reactions that create self-anger or self-hatred or takes the pain to be personal – thus experiencing Dukkha
- Releases the attention from these proliferative thoughts and brings it to the next step
- Relaxes any tension present in the body and the center of that painful feeling as well as any aggravation in the form of energy in the mind associated with the afflictive emotions – hence letting go of Taṇhā and experiencing Nirodha
- Re-smiles to uplift the mind so that it is primed for a more balanced mind
- Returns to a compassionate or loving and kind mindset or a tranquil mind that resulted from relaxing – or further experiencing the Nirodha of Dukkha
- Repeats the whole process again whenever thoughts of self-anger or identification with the pain that create craving arise and utilizing Magga

Sadness and Distress

Sadness and distress can be understood as depression and anxiety. Both depression and anxiety can arise due to various causes and conditions, and between these two ends of a pendulum is an entire spectrum of numerous unwholesome states of mind that are not conducive for the training mind to understand Dukkha, abandon Taṇhā, and experience Nirodha by cultivating Magga. For the sake of deepening the understanding of Dukkha, let us explore these two states of mind and how certain afflictive emotions in between can cause the pendulum to swing one way or the other, causing further craving, aversion, identification and thus further Dukkha. Once there is an understanding, one can use the tools of the Path to let go and experience the pause of that pendulum, the complete extinction which is Nibbāna.

Depression or sadness is primarily rooted in aversion and is an extreme form of pervasive sloth and torpor. The mind makes contact with an unwholesome thought, and the immediate reaction is to push it away and close down to all activities, causing low energy and low mood. It can be a response to various life events – such as the loss of a relationship, one's work, the death of someone close – but it could also be an innate effect of injury to the brain or of certain medications. Abuse at an early stage in life is a major factor. One's self-worth becomes lowered with each exposure to abuse, and there can arise self-hatred and despondency, which gives rise to feeling like life is not worth living, and the mind closes down on any sense of hope or a way out. This makes things less enjoyable and thus one actually feels anhedonia, where there is an emptiness to sensual pleasures and motivation to do anything because the thinking process goes something like, "what's the use?" Note, there is a different in seeing the emptiness of sensual pleasures with wisdom, in which the mind is still inwardly uplifted and motivated with Right Intention, and in seeing the uselessness of sensual pleasures and not seeing a way out and thus having sloth and torpor. In the first case it is the development of the Path and in the second it is the development of unwholesome states and responses, particularly melancholy and hopelessness.

Depression can arise as a response that is learned through behavioral conditioning, meaning one sees the value of being withdrawn at the fear of becoming criticized and starts to make psychological associations between an event and one's confirmation bias that the world is indeed a sad place and there is no way out – with thoughts like, "See, they don't want me to attend the party because I'm a nobody" and so on. Low self-esteem arises out of such circumstances, and self-hatred only deepens the sadness. Certain medications or illnesses too can give rise to depression. As a side effect of medication, depression can resolve itself with the cessation of that medication and as a symptom of certain neurological conditions it can be treated as such or cease as a result of treating the conditions themselves. It can arise due to hereditary causes as well, but these can be managed with wisdom and therapy in the long-term and medication if required in the short term.

The danger of prolonged sadness is twofold. First, if an untrained mind begins to take all of life being this way and takes it personal, such sadness can give rise to a cynical worldview that says, "if people are like this then that means all people are like this and therefore existence is like this and there is no way out," which can then lead to deep pessimism for life. Sadness can also arise out of a desire to hold onto things that were perfect in one's mind at a certain point but no longer are because of the nature of impermanence. This gives rise to regret, nostalgia, and melancholy. Deep sadness can sometimes create bitterness, and a cold heart, which directly opposes two of the three factors of Right Intention – non-ill will and non-cruelty. This bitterness can sometimes manifest in lashing out causing further Dukkha to the mind and to others, and thus one breaks precepts. Depression or sadness can give rise to unwholesome states such as craving, aversion, restlessness, further sloth and torpor and doubt, as well as grief, hatred, bitterness, cynicism, and apathy and these can have interconnections with one another. Ultimately, one is unable to manage the mind with mindfulness or meditation, and there is no perceivable way out of Saṃsāra except suicide to such a mind imbued with this sadness.

Suicidal ideation itself can arise out of various causes and conditions. In the passive sense, it is the mere considering that life is not worth living and therefore one desires death. In the active sense, one thinks about the various methods of suicide and even formulates a plan of action for it. Again, it arises out of many different factors, such as mental disorders, drug and alcohol abuse, societal conditioning, preexisting medical conditions or media influence, but the commonalities include certain painful mental feelings about oneself. One may feel like there is an alarming number of terrible things arising all at once in one's life and therefore the way out of this pressurizing mental pain is to end one's life. One may feel like they are a burden to others or that one is all alone with no one to look towards for emotional support. One is unable to forgive one's past actions and feels like they deserve to be dead or that one feels so filled with sorrow at a loss of a friend, relationship or the death of a loved one, or finances or career, because they've tied their identity so much around these people, situations or things that they feel like ending their own identities through suicide.

Anxiety is a general response or collection of various mechanisms in the mind and body in relation to an experience that is subjectively perceived to be painful. It is a state of intense discomfort and can be part of a nervous disorder. It gives rise to the worry and restlessness that can be uncontrollable for the untrained mind. It can arise out of fear from a perceived threat or as a response to misfortune, such as the loss of friends, bereavement, or a total upheaval of one's life, where mind is unable to cope with the inconstancy of life in general. Uncertainty about the future gives rise to restlessness and this can cause anxiety to become the normal state of mind if there is continual attention given to the dread one has of the future and the inability to assess what could happen, which prompts the mind to fume and proliferate on various what-if scenarios.

Anxiety has many different markers. It can arise as an acute panic attack where one experiences stark unease, palpitation, shortness of breath and sweating. There can be a feeling of loss of control of one's environment and senses and one may feel like they're having a heart attack. Chronic anxiety or general anxiety arises in different ways – the mind is always on edge and the body is restless. One can bite one's nails or tap one's foot or be unable to cope with events through lack of sleep and the constant barrage of thoughts. There may be trouble becoming collected and a sense of dread may take over one's perspective. One's sensory experiences can heighten, and one may exaggerate certain feelings, such as tightness in the chest as an indication of a heart attack. One may feel dizzy, nauseous, have difficulty breathing, shake and sweat. All of these are typical markers of anxiety in general, but the symptoms manifest in different ways.

Anxiety can arise out of Saṅkhāra Dukkha, where there is present in the mind existential dread and a pessimistic attitude toward life. One is unable to see a way out. Fear and terror set in, and it feels claustrophobic. Meeting new people and or being among a large group of people can cause one to feel restless. When going for an interview or facing a crowd, or attending an exam, there can be jitters arising from the fear of the outcome of these events. When having to make a choice and one is unable to after weighing out the pros and cons because of analysis paralysis, anxiety can set in. When there is wrong meditation and mindfulness present, the mind is unable to relax and let go and take personally all thoughts arising and passing away. There can be a sense of impending doom and an inescapable Dukkha where nothing will work to alleviate it. The underlying fetter that causes this is restlessness.

Anxiety can also have genetic or physiological causes. If one has grown up with parents who were constantly on edge or if the household in general was always frantic one is unable to cope and becomes generally anxious. Imbalances of nutrition and intestinal flora can also cause reactions that bring an anxious perspective on events and experiences. Certain medical conditions such as thyroid imbalances, diabetes, deficiencies and strokes as well as cerebrally degenerative illnesses can be factors for anxiety and distress. Of course, too much caffeine, alcohol, or drug abuse in general as well as withdrawal from these substances can lead to a mindset of distress and panic. Defense mechanisms learned early in life along with cognitive distortions where mind takes things personal and colors events through emotional reasoning or makes things seem worse than they really are build up saṅkhāras that can lead to behavioral tendencies towards wrong view, doubt, craving, aversion, and existential craving all rooted in ignorance, meaning not seeing the Four Noble Truths in every given moment. Like depression, depending on the frequency and range of the anxiety, it can lead to suicidal tendencies as well. Anxiety or distress can give rise to more painful states such as restlessness, doubt, ill will, craving, aversion as well as anger, irritation, annoyance and hatred and each of these have interconnections with each other.

Understanding Sadness and Distress with Right Effort

When the mind begins to drift into the past or contemplates and ruminates about the loss one may have experienced in life, whether recently or in the past, and nostalgia, regret, and sadness give way to more depressive thoughts, know this to be the First Noble Truth of Dukkha. When the mind begins to proliferate, entering a vicious whirlpool of non-stop thoughts that gets itself more distraught and depressed, reacting to a situation, whether in the past or in the moment or even contemplating depressive thoughts about the future, know this to be the Second Noble Truth of Taṇhā. When utilizing the Path or the Fourth Noble Truth of Magga via the 6Rs, the mind then enters a balanced state, where no discursive or intrusive thoughts arise, and this is the Third Noble Truth of Nirodha. Whether the mind becomes gloomy or despondent, melancholic or filled with sloth and torpor, one

- Recognizes that depressive thoughts have arisen, which are Dukkha
- Release the attention from these thoughts and directs them to the next step
- Relaxes any Taṇhā in the mind or body by letting go of any tension and experiencing Nirodha
- Re-smiles to uplift the mind
- Returns to a more balanced, wholesome state of mind, further deepening Nirodha
- Repeats whenever needed, thus utilizing Magga

Anytime the mind becomes agitated, where it feels like there are numerous thoughts and there are other symptoms of restlessness arising, escalating into a panic attack or anxiety, know that to be the First Noble Truth of Dukkha. When the mind has aversion by pushing away such thoughts or feelings because it feels uncomfortable and starts to personalize the process by magnifying any pain or the like as a symptom of a worse illness or activity than it actually is, know that to be the Second Noble Truth of Taṇhā. When mind realizes this, takes a pause, relaxes, and uses the 6Rs, one cultivates the Fourth Noble Truth of Magga to return mind to the cessation of Dukka or the Third Noble Truth of Nirodha. One

- Recognizes the anxiety and restlessness as Dukkha
- Releases attention from anxiety and, instead of pushing it away, gently directs mind towards relaxation
- Relaxes body and mind to let go of Taṇhā
- Re-smiles to generate a relaxed, tranquil, and joyful state
- Returns to the relaxed mind born from letting go and continues to experience Nirodha
- Repeats whenever mind drifts away again and thus exercises Magga every time

Remember, if you experience certain symptoms of depression or anxiety that warrant medicinal care and seeking a therapist, by all means, follow the guidance of a licensed medical doctor in the mental health field.

Appiyehi Sampayogo Dukkho, Piyehi Vippayogo Dukkho

Katamo ca, bhikkhave, appiyehi sampayogo dukkho? Idha yassa te honti aniṭṭhā akantā amanāpā rūpā saddā gandhā rasā phoṭṭhabbā dhammā, ye vā panassa te honti anatthakāmā ahitakāmā aphāsukakāmā ayogakkhemakāmā, yā tehi saddhiṁ saṅgati samāgamo samodhānaṁ missībhāvo, ayaṁ vuccati, bhikkhave, appiyehi sampayogo dukkho.

Katamo ca, bhikkhave, piyehi vippayogo dukkho? Idha yassa te honti iṭṭhā kantā manāpā rūpā saddā gandhā rasā phoṭṭhabbā dhammā, ye vā panassa te honti atthakāmā hitakāmā phāsukakāmā yogakkhemakāmā mātā vā pitā vā bhātā vā bhaginī vā mittā vā amaccā vā ñātisālohitā vā, yā tehi saddhiṁ asaṅgati asamāgamo asamodhānaṁ amissībhāvo, ayaṁ vuccati, bhikkhave, piyehi vippayogo dukkho.

And what, monks, is being attached to the unloved? Here, whoever has unwanted, disliked, unpleasant sight-objects, sounds, smells, tastes, tangibles or mind-objects, or whoever encounters ill-wishers, wishers of harm, of discomfort, of insecurity, with whom they have concourse, intercourse, connection, union, that, monks, is called being attached to the unloved.

And what is being separated from the loved? Here, whoever has what is wanted, liked, pleasant sight-objects, sounds, smells, tastes, tangibles or mind-objects, or whoever encounters well-wishers, wishers of good, of comfort, of security, mother or father or brother or sister or younger kinsmen or friends or colleagues or blood-relations, and then is deprived of such concourse, intercourse, connection, or union, that, monks, is called being separated from the loved.

- DN 22, Mahāsatipaṭṭhāna Sutta

Yampicchaṁ Na Labhati Tampi Dukkhaṁ

Katamañca, bhikkhave, yampicchaṁ na labhati tampi dukkhaṁ?

Jātidhammānaṁ, bhikkhave, sattānaṁ evaṁ icchā uppajjati: 'aho vata mayaṁ na jātidhammā assāma, na ca vata no jāti āgaccheyyā'ti. Na kho panetaṁ icchāya pattabbaṁ,

Jarādhammānaṁ, bhikkhave, sattānaṁ evaṁ icchā uppajjati:'aho vata mayaṁ na jarādhammā assāma, na ca vata no jarā āgaccheyyā'ti.Na kho panetaṁ icchāya pattabbaṁ, idampi yampicchaṁ na labhati tampi dukkhaṁ.

Byādhidhammānaṁ, bhikkhave, sattānaṁ evaṁ icchā uppajjati 'aho vata mayaṁ na byādhidhammā assāma, na ca vata no byādhi āgaccheyyā'ti.Na kho panetaṁ icchāya pattabbaṁ, idampi yampicchaṁ na labhati tampi dukkhaṁ.

Maraṇadhammānaṁ, bhikkhave, sattānaṁ evaṁ icchā uppajjati 'aho vata mayaṁ na maraṇadhammā assāma, na ca vata no maraṇaṁ āgaccheyyā'ti.Na kho panetaṁ icchāya pattabbaṁ, idampi yampicchaṁ na labhati tampi dukkhaṁ.

Sokaparidevadukkhadomanassupāyāsadhammānaṁ, bhikkhave, sattānaṁ evaṁ icchā uppajjati 'aho vata mayaṁ na sokaparidevadukkhadomanassupāyāsadhammā assāma, na ca vata no sokaparidevadukkhadomanassupāyāsaā āgaccheyyun'ti. Na kho panetaṁ icchāya pattabbaṁ, idampi yampicchaṁ na labhati tampi dukkhaṁ.

And what is not getting what one wants?

In beings subject to birth, monks, this wish arises: "Oh, that we were not subject to birth, that we might not come to birth!" But this cannot be gained by wishing. That is not getting what one wants.

In beings subject to aging, monks, this wish arises: "Oh, that we were not subject to aging, that we might not come to aging!" But this cannot be gained by wishing. That is not getting what one wants.

In beings subject to death, monks, this wish arises: "Oh that we were not subject to death, that we might not come to death!" But this cannot be gained by wishing. That is not getting what one wants.

In beings subject to sorrow, monks, this wish arises: "Oh that we were not subject to sorrow, that we might not come to sorrow!" But this cannot be gained by wishing. That is not getting what one wants.

In beings subject to lamentation, monks, this wish arises: "Oh that we were not subject to lamentation, that we might not come to lamentation!" But this cannot be gained by wishing. That is not getting what one wants.

In beings subject to pain, monks, this wish arises: "Oh that we were not subject to pain, that we might not come to pain!" But this cannot be gained by wishing. That is not getting what one wants.

In beings subject to sadness, monks, this wish arises: "Oh that we were not subject to sadness, that we might not come to sadness!" But this cannot be gained by wishing. That is not getting what one wants.

In beings subject to distress, monks, this wish arises: "Oh that we were not subject to distress, that we might not come to distress!" But this cannot be gained by wishing. That is not getting what one wants.

- DN 22, Mahāsatipaṭṭhāna Sutta

Union with the Unpleasant and Separation from the Pleasant

All experience that arises happens through a dichotomy. There is a signal and there is a receiver. The intermediary between these adds to a trichotomy by which there can be a further projection of concepts to an experience. This dyad is that of the twelve sense bases, the āyatanas. An āyatana is a plane, sphere, or base, and can be used interchangeably between the internal sense bases and the external sense bases, and beyond that āyatana refers to the states of meditation known as Infinite Space, Infinite Consciousness, Nothingness, and Neither Perception nor non-Perception. The twelve sense bases are the internal – the eyes, ears, nose, tongue, body, and mind – and the external – forms, sounds, smells, tastes, tangibles, and thoughts or, more broadly, mind objects. Even though thoughts seem to appear internally, they are separate from mind and so they are objects of the mind.

Now what about the triad? This is where manasikāra, or attention, comes in. It's through the process of attention that there is a connection made between the internal and external sense bases. Attention is a factor of nāma, or mind or the mental aspects of the framework of the way interaction is made between the world and the body, which is rupā. Nāmarupā is the fourth link in the process of Dependent Origination and is the storehouse of components of faculties through which one experiences feeling, perception, contact, intention and attention. Now, when photons bounce of a form and traverse to the photoreceptors in the eye the meeting of the two brings up eye-consciousness, or when soundwaves vibrate the auditory receptors in the ear the meeting of the two brings up ear-consciousness, or when odor molecules touch the olfactory system in the nose the meeting of the two bring up nose-consciousness, or when taste molecules impact the taste buds in the tongue the meeting of the two brings up tongue-consciousness, or when there is air pressure or temperature touching the body the meeting of the two brings up body-consciousness, or finally when a thought impacts the mind the meeting of the two brings up mind-consciousness.

The process of attention is consciousness arising from the impact of the elements of the dyad. Cognition of the stimulation of the internal sense bases is consciousness and facilitated by attention. When the three – the external base, the internal base, and the corresponding cognition of the internal sense base – meet together, this forms the process of phassa, or contact, which is the sixth link in the process of Dependent Origination. There is then a felt experience, which is vedanā, the seventh link.

Through this perception gives meaning to the experience as pleasant, unpleasant, or neutral. If the mind has already been fettered by craving, conceit, and ignorance, then whatever experience arises will already have the potential for the eighth link to arise – taṇhā – that is craving or aversion or taking the experience to belong to a sense of personal self. This then gives rise to the further links of upādāna, or clinging, bhava, or being, and jāti, or rebirth, which bring about Dukkha. In reality, Dukkha is present in every link of Dependent Origination, and as we will see, Dukkha manifests even in the experience of contact, feeling, and perception as an effect of previous choices, which we will explore further in the next section.

When it comes to the unpleasant experiences, they arise because of unpleasant feeling – the eye makes contact with disgusting or horrifying sight, the ear makes contact with loud and disturbing sounds, the nose makes contact with malodors, the tongue makes contact with nausea-inducing tastes, the body makes contact with uncomfortable touches, and mind makes contact with anxious or depressive thoughts – and they are the truth of those moments. That is the Dukkha in those moment. This extends to having to deal with other beings who don't have our best interests at heart, who you may consider, or they may consider themselves, your enemy and are obstacles in your path to freedom and peace. Encounters with people like this happen at any point in one's day, and that is Dukkha.

Say you're walking down the street and talking with your friend. You don't notice what's directly in front of your feet and you step on some dog feces. The sight and smell of it is associating with the unpleasant. At the same time, a garbage trucks whip by and starts honking loudly – now there is a terrible, irritating sound that impacts your ears. As you tried to wipe the feces off of your shoes, another pedestrian knocks into you, and you fall over and now you experience bodily discomfort and pain. Then, your mind gets irritated, and you lash out at the person. The other person is having a bad day as well and you lashing out is the final straw for them, and in your anger, they assault you. All of these are unpleasant experiences and therefore Dukkha.

Separation from the pleasant is the Dukkha of change, or Vipariṇāma Dukkha. Here your encounter pleasant sights, sounds, smells, tastes, tangibles, and thoughts, or you're having a good time with your friends and loved ones, laughing and in joy, but then a stimulus changes that. When before you were enjoying sensual pleasures and with loved ones, something triggers a cessation to that. In the case of being with loved ones, death or someone choosing to move away or break up a relationship, can be this Dukkha of separation of what was previously pleasant. When you're watching a wonderful movie and really enjoying it and suddenly the power goes out, now you're no longer able to finish the movie. When you're in the middle of a wonderful dinner, savoring every morsel and suddenly your phone rings and it's an emergency – your boss wants you to come into work, or someone is hurt and requires assistance – this is separation from the smells and tastes and wonderful mental feeling. When you're meditating and on your object of meditation, enjoying the feeling of joy and comfort that arises, and then someone knocks on the door, catapulting your mind's attention from the pleasant feeling, this is separation from the pleasant.

What one has to understand is, there is Dukkha present in every moment and if mind allows it to pervade the mind with craving or aversion, in that if one is having a bad day or if one is enjoying the most wonderful day and it all comes crashing down and in either case the mind takes all of the elements of changes personally, there is craving and thus further Dukkha arises.

Understanding Union and Separation with Right Effort

Let's use the example of walking down the street to see how one can understand Dukkha and then abandon further Dukkha from arising through the Path and finally experience cessation of any further Dukkha. Now, when you're walking down the street and you accidentally step on dog feces, and you see the sight and there is a smell to it, this is the First Noble Truth of Dukkha. If you notice, your mind becomes irritated; with mindfulness, you let go of the Second Noble Truth of Taṇhā in the form of that irritation. You utilize the Fourth Noble Truth of Magga by letting go and experience the Third Noble Truth of Nirodha. You forgive yourself if you have to and you laugh it off.

Taking this example further, say you hear the Dukkha of the garbage truck honking, and your mind latches on to that and starts to hate it, you let go of that Taṇhā of hatred by using the

6Rs that encapsulate the Path and find relief of Nirodha from that honking bothering you anymore. Now the pedestrian accidentally knocks you over. This is Dukkha. You become distraught and want to lash out at them – this is Taṇhā. You notice the craving arising and let go using the 6Rs – the Path – and experience the Nirodha of the craving and hence further Dukkha, and you have compassion and forgiveness towards the stranger. Now the stranger is sorry and instead of punching you, they apologize and make sure you're okay. In acting in a wholesome manner, you prevented further Dukkha and Taṇhā for yourself as well as for the stranger, and thus they don't experience unwholesome states or actions.

To understand the Dukkha of union with the unpleasant, whatever it might be, and then let go of any craving that can cause further Dukkha to arise, one

- Recognizes that the mind has become displeased with a situation, whether it is a sensory experience or a mental one, thus seeing the First Noble Truth of Dukkha
- Releases the attention away from that experience and the mind's reaction to it and brings it back to the present moment
- Relaxes the tension present in mind and/or body which is a manifestation of the Second Noble Truth of Taṇhā, and experiences the Third Noble Truth of Nirodha
- Re-smiles to uplift the mind and replace the unwholesome states with wholesome qualities

- Returns mind back to the presence of awareness from the Relax step and thus strengthens the experience of the Third Noble Truth of Nirodha

- Repeats whenever mind gravitates towards craving or personalizing the situation and therefore utilizes the Fourth Noble Truth of Magga

Let's now illustrate how one can understand letting go of separation with what is loved. Say you have just made a delicious meal and are about to sit down to enjoy it. You're expecting it to be good, and in fact, you're delighting in the flavors even before you've enjoyed it with a wonderful aroma. The fact is craving has arisen in the form of anticipation for the food. Now, as you sit down, the phone rings, and it's someone in need of immediate assistance on the other line – it could be an emergency at work or among friends or something else – and you realize you have to leave and won't be able to finish your meal. You've been separated from having a nice meal in peace and quiet and mental pleasure. This separation is Dukkha. The craving you had earlier, and the irritation you may feel, which creates further unease in mind is Taṇhā. If you choose to see this with mindfulness and realize that this is an opportunity to help someone in need, you let go of the irritation and experience Nirodha. The use of mindfulness and letting go is rooted in Magga. So, using the 6Rs, what you effectively do is

- Recognize the irritation from the separation from your meal, which is the Dukkha

- Release your attention from taking it personally and bring it to relaxing the mind and/or body

- Relax any tension in mind and/or body as a manifestation of Taṇhā and feel the relief in that moment that is Nirodha

- Re-smile to uplift the mind and reframe your perspective – this is an opportunity to help someone in need and exercise loving-kindness and compassion

- Return to the feeling of relaxation and further deepen the Nirodha with loving-kindness and compassion

- Repeat whenever irritation about the situation arises, thus continually cultivating Magga

Wisdom informs the practice and practice develops wisdom. Continually cultivating the Path through mindfulness, seeing craving arising, abandoning that craving and experiencing relief – the cessation of suffering – one develops wisdom. One is able to peel away the layers of ignorance every time one sees the union with the unpleasant and separation from the pleasant as being impermanent, and therefore not worth holding onto since holding onto the experience causes further Dukkha, and seeing it as impersonal, meaning you didn't have a say in whether something happened a certain way or didn't happen in another way.

This insight into the tilakkhaṇa is nurtured through careful observation and letting the vision of it arise on its own with a collected mind. When this happens, it is easier to let go of any personalizing or identification with any of the twelve āyatanas.

Doing so, one doesn't have craving and therefore the possibility of further Dukkha is extinguished right there and then. With every implementation of the 6Rs one continues to retrain the mind so that it takes things less personally and ultimately takes nothing personally and understands the impermanence and Dukkha-inducing nature of all things if reacted to in an unwholesome way.

For the liberated mind all that arises like sights, sounds, smells, tastes, tangibles, mind-objects, as well as the experiences that arise from them are automatically seen for what they truly are – in flux, prone to cause further Dukkha with wrong attention, and impersonal processes.

Inability to Manifest a Wish and Kamma

The essential understanding of the Dhamma is causation. There are certain causes that give arise to certain effects. Correlation is when one sees a connection between two events, but they are not always cause and effect. The events may arise separately from separate causes and conditions, but the correlation is seeing that when something happens, something else happens. In the case of cause and effect, there is contact and thus there arises a feeling. It cannot be any other way. When the contact ceases, the feeling ceases. An absurd example of correlation is "when ice cream sales increase, the murder rate increases," but one event doesn't cause the other. They seem to have a connection by a third factor that when temperatures rise people tend to buy more ice cream and hotter environments can be an irritant to a person's frame of mind. Now, a coincidence is what people see as something that arose due to chance and thus the coincidence was a happy accident, like someone thinking of a friend and at the same time they receive a phone call. Seeing in this way at the extreme end can lead to the belief in fatalism, that all is left to a supreme creator and what must happen will happen without any interference of choice, and at the other extreme there is the belief that this is due to synchronicity, where one has a say in how to manifest reality with one's thoughts alone.

This little primer is meant for one to understand that the concept of wishing for something and that it happens because of one's innate manifestative abilities is rooted in a deep sense of self. The truth is if you were to think of acquiring a blue elephant right now, it wouldn't just happen. That's now how Saṃsāra works. Now if you really wanted a blue elephant, you would take certain actions, which cause certain effects, all that lead to the acquisition of the blue elephant (provided there is such a thing as a blue elephant). What is being illustrated here is that all things that are experienced in this moment have come about due to certain actions and are the effects of certain causes. This is kamma. One does something wholesome and later on one sees the wholesome effect of that action. This is the understanding of action and consequence. If one were to experience Dukkha in the forms already discussed and then had the wish, "let it not be so," that wouldn't put an end to Dukkha. In fact, the mere wishing of it to end is the Taṇhā that causes further Dukkha. Instead, one sees with wisdom and abandons the initial cause of the Dukkha, which would invariably be some form of craving. Letting this go, one doesn't experience that Dukkha any further. Everything experienced in the way of Dukkha and its factors already mentioned happens due to a series of causes and conditions and to take them personal and wish they didn't arise is another form of Dukkha. Because they arose due to certain causes and conditions, they can cease due to another set of causes and conditions, or the cessation of the previous causes and conditions.

This brings us to the understanding of kamma. Kamma is bound in intention, which means the actions we produce arise due to intentions and those intention arise when there is contact with the world. For example, it's a hot day. You see the shade of a tree. The seeing of the shade brings up the intention to walk to the tree to get some relief from the hot day. The Buddha also stated that kamma is quite deep and complex and to see all the strands of kamma is quite difficult to do, and these strands are intertwined with other factors including climate, the political, societal, and other forms of environment, other beings' actions, and one's internal state of health, among others. To simplify this understanding, let's look at how kamma has a delineation point between what is old kamma, which is the effect of a previous set of actions committed in the past, and what is new kamma, which is a set of actions that create a corresponding effect in the future, by looking at excerpts from three suttas.

Katamañca, bhikkhave, purāṇakammaṁ? Cakkhu, bhikkhave, purāṇakammaṁ abhisaṅkhataṁ abhisañcetayitaṁ vedaniyaṁ daṭṭhabbaṁ

Katamañca, bhikkhave, navakammaṁ? Yaṁ kho, bhikkhave, etarahi kammaṁ karoti kāyena vācāya manasā, idaṁ vuccati, bhikkhave, navakammaṁ.

Katamo ca, bhikkhave, kammanirodho? Yo kho, bhikkhave, kāyakammavacīkammamanokammassa nirodhā vimuttiṁ phusati, ayaṁ vuccati, bhikkhave, kammanirodho.

Katamā ca, bhikkhave, kammanirodhagāminī paṭipadā? Ayameva ariyo aṭṭhaṅgiko maggo

And what, bhikkhus, is old kamma? The eye is old kamma, to be seen as generated and fashioned by volition, as something to be felt. This is called old kamma.

And what, bhikkhus is new kamma? Whatever action one does now by body, speech, or mind. This is called new kamma.

And what, bhikkhus, is the cessation of kamma? When one reaches liberation through the cessation of bodily action, verbal action, and mental action, this is called the cessation of kamma.

And what, bhikkhus, is the way leading to the cessation of kamma? It is this Noble Eightfold Path.

- SN 35.146, Kammanirodha Sutta

Cetanāhaṁ, bhikkhave, kammaṁ vadāmi. Cetayitvā kammaṁ karoti— kāyena vācāya manasā.

Katamo ca, bhikkhave, kammānaṁ nidānasambhavo? Phasso, bhikkhave, kammānaṁ nidānasambhavo.

Katamo ca, bhikkhave, kammanirodho? Phassanirodho, bhikkhave, kammanirodho. Ayameva ariyo aṭṭhaṅgiko maggo kammanirodhagāminī paṭipadā

It is volition, bhikkhus, that I call kamma. For having willed, one acts by body, speech, or mind.

And what is the source and origin of kamma? Contact is its source and origin.

And what, bhikkhus, is the cessation of kamma? With the cessation of contact there is cessation of kamma. This noble eightfold path is the way leading to the cessation of kamma.

- AN 6.63, Nibbedhika Sutta

So navañca kammaṁ na karoti, purāṇañca kammaṁ phussa phussa byantīkaroti. Sandiṭṭhikā nijjarā akālikā ehipassikā opaneyyikā paccattaṁ veditabbā viññūhīti.

He does not create any new kamma, and he terminates the old kamma, having contacted it again and again. The wearing away is directly visible, immediate, inviting one to come and see, applicable, to be personally experienced by the wise.

- AN 3.74, Nigaṇṭha Sutta

Dukkha is kamma, both old and new. Everything one has experienced in the way of the sense bases and the sensual pleasures or displeasures up to this exact moment of reading is old Dukkha, or old kamma. In the context of Dependent Origination, this means, with each link possessing intrinsic Dukkha, from ignorance to formations to consciousness to mind and body to the sense bases to contact, feeling and perception with perception being tied to feeling, all of them up until here are old Dukkha and old kamma. Now, if one reacts with craving, clinging, and being, this gives rise to the rebirth of action, and the whole mass of new Dukkha, to be experienced as old Dukkha in another moment, perhaps the next or in a series of moments much later. Drinking alcohol all night long and experiencing a hangover the next day exemplifies this understanding. First, one is faced with the craving for alcohol. The presence of alcohol made contact with the sense bases, which provided an intention to drink. All this is old kamma. Then, having craved the alcohol, there is the arising of new kamma in the form of the hangover. This is also now the old Dukkha and old kamma of the next morning. If one chooses to react in a way that causes one to experience further Dukkha, then one is creating a new kamma. A more wholesome and supramundane example of this would be while one is meditating – when you are faced with hindrances, which is Dukkha, and that is old kamma as a result of having broken precepts in the past, and if one sees this, accepts it, and lets it go by using the 6Rs, the hindrance as old kamma will dissipate.

Old Dukkha is all that one has inherited from previous choices, and this Dukkha is perpetuated into new Dukkha by new intention and choices in a moment after the link of feeling is experienced in the process of Dependent Origination. Here old Dukkha and old kamma can cease with wisdom and the Path through the 6R process. To hammer in this understanding, every factor of Dukkha is an experience to be felt. Rebirth, illness, aging, death, sorrow, lamentation, pain, sadness and distress, union with the unpleasant, separation with the pleasant, and not getting what one wishes – these are all vedanā or feeling. They are experiences. Now, if you want to perpetuate them, causing further Dukkha, you can choose to take them personally and have an attitude of craving or aversion as a reaction to them. Doing so, you will then create clinging and being, leading to a new action that propagates new variations of that Dukkha as a new vedanā or feeling.

Understanding Kamma with Right Effort

What is the way out of this cycle? The Path – understanding that such Dukkha in the form of vedanā has arisen and that craving for it or aversion against it or taking it personally has become a response to this vedanā. Instead of letting that continue, one lets go of the link of craving with Right Effort and comes back to a more balanced mind. Kamma is to be terminated at feeling, but if one continues to take it personally, it will get renewed. If one relaxes and lets it happen without any craving, conceit, or ignorance, with complete mindfulness and understanding, then that kamma or Dukkha is worn away bit by bit as is mentioned in the Nigaṇṭha Sutta. It's not that the kamma will completely be disintegrated every time – it may manifest in various ways, but if it does arise again, it won't be as strong the first time and will continue to weaken every time one 6Rs it until there is nothing left of it, due also to the new patterns of response to that kamma as it is losing its hold as an object of attachment. Let's look at how this process occurs with Right Effort. One

- Recognizes Dukkha and kamma in the form of a vedanā, seeing it as something being felt and nothing more, instead of continuing to let mind take it personally

- Releases the attention from this experience and directs it to mind and body

- Relaxes any Taṇhā present in the form of mental or physical tension and experiences Nirodha – here, with the cessation of craving is the cessation of further Dukkha and new kamma as well as the cessation of old kamma for this time around

- Re-smiles to uplift the mind with joy, comfort, and tranquility

- Returns to a balanced state of mind that further deepens the experience of Nirodha

- Repeats whenever old kamma arises again and takes it personally

Pañcupādānakkhandhā

Katame ca, bhikkhave, saṅkhittena pañcupādānakkhandhā dukkhā? Seyyathidaṁ—rūpupādānakkhandho, vedanupādānakkhandho, saññupādānakkhandho, saṅkhārupādānakkhandho, viññāṇupādānakkhandho. Ime vuccanti, bhikkhave, saṅkhittena pañcupādānakkhandhā dukkhā.

And how, monks, in short, are the five aggregates subject to clinging? They are as follows: the aggregate form that is subject to clinging, the aggregate of feeling that is subject to clinging, the aggregate of perception that is subject to clinging, the aggregate of formations that are subject to clinging, the aggregate of consciousness that is subject to clinging. These are, in short, the five aggregates that is subject to clinging that are suffering.

- DN 22, Mahāsatipaṭṭhāna Sutta

The five aggregates and the five aggregates subject to clinging are identical –form, feeling, perception, formations, and consciousness – except, as the latter's name suggests, these aggregates are affected by clinging. What that clinging is, we will explore a little further. Let's understand what these aggregates are in the context of conditioned experience. Aggregate comes from the Pali khanda. Khanda refers to a heap or a portion. It's essentially dividing the ways in which conditioned reality is experienced, and these divisions are classified similarly to the way nāmarupā is divided – indeed, it can be said they are one and the same. These divisions provide one the ability to look at conditioned reality through a specialized context, a microscopic lens for understanding reality. It is through the five aggregates that Dukkha arises, by their very nature of being impermanent, but also because clinging to them or from them gives rise to Dukkha as well. They are even broken down even further by way of sensory experiences in relation to each of the aggregates. Let's understand each aggregate one by one.

Form Aggregate

Rupā khanda of the form aggregate is made from the four great elements. The four great elements in Ancient Indian thought are earth, water, air, and fire. These can be contextualized in our current understanding of a matter, which corresponds beautifully with the four great elements. The earth element corresponds to solid matter, water to liquid matter, air to gaseous matter, and fire to plasma matter. Plasma here doesn't refer to the plasma in blood but rather ionized gas. When gas becomes hot enough, it is subject to electricity and magnetism. For the sake of simplicity, one can understand fire to be equivalent to plasma, and this can also be equivalized to the electrical impulses in the body through neural pathways that send and receive messages.

All of Saṃsāra is made up of these four great elements in one way or another, and our own bodies are made up of the four great elements. Therefore, form isn't just our bodies which can include external form and internal form such as our organs, but can be other beings' bodies, insentient matter, whether they are close to us or far away from us, whether they were there before or are present now, or they will be in the future, whether they are subtle or grossly perceivable, whether they are inferior in quality or superior. For the sake of understanding subjective experience, we will stick with seeing the form that is our body. This body requires nourishment, and so it is understood that the body depends on food for its sustenance and growth, and without it the body will eventually wither away. Of course, the body is also dependent upon craving in that it is through craving that one objectifies the body and makes it more than what it is really is – insentient matter, a corpse-to-be that is animated via contact, feeling, perception, intention, and consciousness. The six sense bases are made of form. In this context, then, there is an interdependence between form and contact. Without contact, there can be no feeling, perception, intention, or cognition to animate the body, but that contact requires a medium, which is the six sense bases, and thus that contact arises on the basis of form. Craving can build up to an unhealthy level when there is a lack of mindfulness of eating, for example; then the mind ceases the process through Attention Rooted in Reality and utilizing the Path.

Feeling Aggregate

Vedanā or feeling is the experience that arises based on contact with one or more of the six sense bases and feeling can be divided into up to one hundred and eight types, but this is something we will discuss in detail when we get to the chapter on Vedanā as a link of Dependent Origination. For now, we understand feeling to be of three types – pleasant, unpleasant, or neutral. Feeling is an experience that is felt – it can be a sensory experience, or it can be a mental experience. The experiencing of seeing a movie, hearing a song, tasting food, smelling fragrances, feeling hot or cold, or of a mental feeling like having loving-kindness or thinking about something in the past are all feeling. In other words, there is feeling dependent on eye contact and ear contact. Feeling, just like form, can be understood as being a feeling from the past, present, or future, a feeling that arises presently and is thus considered near, or a feeling that one considers when thinking of a friend who is halfway around the world is the feeling that is far connected to the thought of that friend, being subtle in its quality or immediately and grossly perceivable or inferior or superior in quality, meaning a feeling that can be limited by boundaries or time or it can be limitless such as the experience of Infinite Space or seeing endless past lives. Without contact, there can be no feeling, so with the cessation of contact, there is the cessation of feeling. The way leading to the cessation of feeling is the implementation of the Path.

Perception Aggregate

Saññа, or perception, is rooted in memory. It is the learned knowledge of concepts and what something is in relation to an experience or an object of experience. For example, one learns the different colors – blue, yellow, red, white, and so on – and upon having learned them, they are now known and within the mind's memory bank. The next time one sees these colors, there is an immediate recognition of them. In other words, perception is re-cognizing something after having first cognized it through learning. Further perception may color emotions dependent upon formations. For example, one perceives someone didn't hear them call their name, and one immediately thinks the person has ignored them, and therefore, one is dismayed because of that perception. However, then they perceive actually the person had small earbuds in their ear while listening to music, and so one becomes embarrassed and realizes the other person was not ignoring them. Concepts of convention are rooted in perception as well. For example, a specific chair designates a certain place in a company boardroom. If one takes these perceptions personally, it can cause all sorts of mental proliferations that can lead to craving and hence further Dukkha.

Perception is tied to feeling and arises from contact. Therefore, there are perceptions of form, sound, taste, smell, bodily sensations, and mental phenomena. The feeling is the experience, while the recognition of it as pleasant, unpleasant, or neutral is the perception. The experience of heat is feeling while recognizing it to be hot is perception. The experience of seeing a tree is feeling while recognizing it to be a birch tree is perception. The experience of hearing a symphony is feeling while recognizing it as Ode to Joy is perception. The experience of smelling perfume is feeling while recognizing it as Calvin Klein's Eternity brand is perception. The experience of tasting food is feeling while recognizing it as sweet, spicy, or the like, or even that is lasagna one is eating is perception. The experience of thinking about the past is feeling while recognizing it as a thought about the first time one went on a family trip, and the emotions associated with that memory is perception. So, as soon as contact arises, feeling co-arises with perception, and when contact ceases so do the feeling and perception. The way to cease perception is through the Path if one recognizes craving, aversion or identification present in it. We explore perception deeper in the chapter on nāmarupā.

Formations Aggregate

Saṅkhāras or formations are used in the context of volition and intention when they are understood as an aggregate. Formations have various meanings depending on the context, but they are primarily associated with intention, the forerunner and cause of consciousness in Dependent Origination, constructions and constructors of experience, and are generally also translated as conditions. We will explore them as a separate and elaborated subject in the chapter on Saṅkhāra. Here the Buddha has explained formations, in the context of the aggregate, as being of six types, which is to say – formations regarding forms, sounds, odors, tastes, bodily sensations, and mental phenomena. When there is contact with the six sense bases, there is feeling and perception, and from there is an intention to do express speech, take an action or to further reflect. For example, one recalls a friend talking about a movie they saw just the other day. The thought makes contact with mind, and there is the feeling of thinking about the movie and the perception of the movie's name and so on. Then, mental formations arise to further consider about the movie, then physical formations arise to walk to one's computer or to find one's smartphone, and then verbal formations arise to consider calling another friend and asking them if they want to join in going to the movie theater.

Formations are quite complex to understand but the best way to see them in the view of choice and intention. Making a choice in the present moment is dependent on previous formations and that choice will bring up a new set of formation. Formations being dependent on contact, when contact ceases formations cease. If formations are fettered by craving and hindered by ignorance, then the intention to do something will have conceit and there could be a potential of craving arising after feeling and perception. For that reason, any time one becomes mindful and abandons craving, they reformat formations for the next choice so that less potential for craving arises in relation to that particular feeling and perception. The way leading to the cessation of such formations rooted in ignorance is the Path.

Consciousness Aggregate

Vijñāna or consciousness is an elusive subject because of its many connotations. It is understood in the context of the aggregates and within the quantum framework of Dependent Origination as cognition and within the cosmic framework of rebirth from one lifetime to another as consciousness that transports formations from life to another and ceases to give rise to a new consciousness established at the moment of conception. Like formations, perception, and feeling, we will explore consciousness on a deeper level in the chapter dedicated to the link of vijñāna. As an aggregate, consciousness or cognition is that which first learns something before it comes a perception to be accessed as memory. For example, you put your hand on the stove fire for the first time and notice it burns. There is cognition of fire as being hot and painful to the body, but when you see that fire can keep you warm on a cold day and cook your food, there's also cognition of the utility of fire. Cognition is also the bare awareness of something. So, when there is feeling – that is a sensual mental experience – there is the bare awareness or knowing of it, and then the perception of it arises. That is why consciousness, feeling, and perception are tied together.

Cognition is divided into six parts, based on the awareness of the six sense bases. Contact is the trifecta of an internal sense base, an external sense base or object, and the corresponding sense consciousness or the awareness of that sense. Therefore, there is eye consciousness, ear consciousness, nose consciousness, tongue consciousness, body consciousness, and mind consciousness. Cognition is dependent upon the factors of contact, feeling, perception, intention, and attention in nāmarupā but is also what gives rise to nāmarupā. This will be explored further but for the purpose of the consciousness aggregate understand that consciousness will arise when it is established through mind and body while also giving awareness of mind and body. On the macro level, consciousness gives rise to nāmarupā at conception and then is tied to nāmarupā and arises dependent upon an experience felt by the nāmarupā.

Where the factors of nāmarupā flow, there a corresponding consciousness will arise. When these factors in nāmarupā cease, that corresponding consciousness ceases as well. If the consciousness is activated by fettered formations, meaning they are conditioned by ignorance and tainted with craving or conceit, then such consciousness too will be tainted and therefore will give rise to fettered mentality which influences the experience of contact as having a sense of "I am" and the proclivity towards craving after vedanā. In order to cease such consciousness, one ceases the fettered factors of mentality through the use of the Path.

Understanding the Clinging in Aggregates with Right Effort

Taññeva nu kho, ayye, upādānaṁ te pañcupādānakkhandhā udāhu aññatra pañcahupādānakkhandhehi upādānan"ti?

Na kho, āvuso visākha, taññeva upādānaṁ te pañcupādānakkhandhā, nāpi aññatra pañcahupādānakkhandhehi upādānaṁ. Yo kho, āvuso visākha, pañcasu upādānakkhandhesu chandarāgo taṁ tattha upādānan"ti.

"Lady, is that clinging the same as these five aggregates affected by clinging, or is the clinging something apart from the five aggregates affected by clinging?"

"Friend Visākha, that clinging is neither the same as these five aggregates affected by clinging nor is clinging something apart from the five aggregates affected by clinging. It is the desire and lust in regard to the five aggregates affected by clinging that is the clinging there."

- MN 44, Cūḷavedalla Sutta

If the clinging aspect of the five aggregates were the same as the five aggregates themselves then there would be no way to eradicate clinging without cease the five aggregates themselves, but the clinging isn't separate from the five aggregates either because if the clinging was separate then that would be there would be a separate aggregate of clinging and one would just need look at that and abandon it without dealing with the five aggregates. The clinging is intertwined with each of the five aggregates by way of the fetters of craving and aversion present in the formations, which then continue down the line of Dependent Origination and thus cause craving, clinging, being, and rebirth and therefore new Dukkha to arise.

When there is a pleasant experience in dependence on form, feeling, perception, formations, or consciousness and that experience is taken personal, which then strengthens the formations fettered by ignorance, craving, and conceit, then there is the cause for renewal of being and Dukkha. When the aggregates are not seen for what they are – Anicca, Dukkha, and

Anatta – then there arises ignorance, dependent upon the taints of sensual craving, being, and ignorance. From this the fettered formations are activated giving rise to the potential for one to cling to the aggregates as self and then cause bhava and jāti. Therefore, the way to remove the upādāna or clinging that the aggregates are affected by is through Attention Rooted in Reality, mindfulness, and wisdom. When an experience arises that brings up the mindfulness of form, feeling, perception, formations in the form of intention or volition, or consciousness, one sees right then and there the experience as well as the aggregate it is dependent upon is impermanent, Dukkha, and impersonal.

When one identifies with form, one's body, that identification is the First Noble Truth of Dukkha. When one has that tension in mind or body present because of the identification process and there is craving or aversion present that is the Second Noble Truth of Taṇhā. If one abandons this through the Fourth Noble Truth of Magga, then one experiences the Third Noble Truth of Nirodha and ceases identifying with form.

When one experiences a feeling and sees it as self in way or another or takes it personally, this is the First Noble Truth of Dukkha. If one craves for further experience to try to continue that feeling or wants to push it away through aversion that is the Second Noble Truth of Dukkha. If one recognizes this and lets this go through the Fourth Noble Truth of Magga and experiences the cessation of that craving, this is the Third Noble Truth of Nirodha.

When one perceives an experiences and projects onto it the sense of "I am" this is the First Noble Truth of Dukkha. When one craves for something based on that perception, this is the Second Noble Truth of Dukkha. If one sees this and abandons the clinging to that perception as "I am" that is the Fourth Noble Truth of Magga and one experiences the cessation of identity, the Third Noble Truth of Nirodha.

When one intends with the idea that same conceit of "I am" then that is the identity rooted in the First Noble Truth of Dukkha. When one then attaches to that intention as self and craves for it to come to fruition, this is the Second Noble Truth of Dukkha. When one abandons the identification with the formation aggregate through intention and sees it as impersonal, one utilizes the Fourth Noble Truth of Magga and experiences relief in the form of the Third Noble Truth of Nirodha.

Finally, when one what cognizes and takes that object of cognition and the cognitive process itself as self, which is the First Noble Truth of Dukkha. When one when craves for what one cognizes by personalizing consciousness, there is present the Second Noble Truth of Tanha. When one lets go through the process of the Fourth Noble Truth of Magga, one experiences relief that is total cessation – the Third Noble Truth of Nirodha.

Let's understand this from the scope of the 6R process. One

- Recognizes when one identifies with one or more of the aggregates and the experiences dependent upon them - Dukkha

- Releases their attention away from them and bring them to relaxation

- Relaxes any tension – Taṇhā - associated with the identification of these experiences and the aggregates, and thus realizes cessation – Nirodha
- Re-smiles and uplifts the mind
- Returns to observing the experiences and their causal aggregates as impermanent, not worth holding onto, and impersonal
- Repeats whenever mind forgets this wisdom and continues to identify with the aggregates

We have now covered the breadth of Dukkha as it has been elucidated by the Buddha and his disciples in various suttas – ageing, illness, death, sorrow, lamentation, pain, sadness, distress and the five aggregates subject to clinging. Jāti, or rebirth, which is a part of this enumeration but deserves its own progressive elaboration will be discussed in the upcoming chapter.

This is the end of the link of 'Dukkha' book .

Made in the USA
Las Vegas, NV
19 October 2022

57734026R00066